BIBLIOTHECA NEERLANDICA

A Library of Classics of Dutch and Flemish Literature

MEDIAEVAL NETHERLANDS RELIGIOUS LITERATURE

MEDIAEVAL NETHERLANDS RELIGIOUS LITERATURE

Translated and Introduced

by

E. COLLEDGE

WALTHAM FOREST PUBLIC LIBRARIES

SYTHOFF LEYDEN / HEINEMANN LONDON
LONDON HOUSE & MAXWELL NEW YORK
1965

Published with the aid of the Prince Bernhard Fund

First published 1965

SPECIAL
SUBJECT 865-7388

WALTHAM FOREST
PUBLIC LIBRARIES

2414

RS 17020

W0010765LB

Library of Congress Catalog Card Number 65-12916

© *A. W.Sijthoff's Uitgeversmaatschappij, N,V. 1964*

No part of this book may be reproduced in any form, by print, photoprint, micro-film or any other means without written permission from the publishers

Printed in the Netherlands by A. W. Sythoff, Printing Division, Leyden

CONTENTS

INTRODUCTION

*It could be said that it is pleonastic to call any medieval European li-
terature 'religious', because there is none which does not in some way
reflect the all-pervading teachings of the Christian faith. The great
Jesuit historian Thurston made this point with admirable succinctness,
writing of a strange pseudo-Christ whose antics are recorded in English
chronicles of the early thirteenth century, when he designates them as
'... some sort of contortionist's or mountebank's trick which took a
religious colour chiefly because the ideas and interests of that age cen-
tred round religious themes'. Though it may seem to superficial ob-
servers that there is no justification, other than that of mere chronology,
for including in the same volume the* Letters *of Hadewijch and* Mary
of Nijmeghen, *the times in which these two authors wrote did impose upon their work a unifying quality, since both were written in
the knowledge that they could appeal to a profound and general assent
to the truths of the Christian faith.*

*The origins of medieval Dutch literature are obscure and for the
most part lost, but it is manifest from the earliest verse which has been
preserved, such as the* Eneide *of the Limburg poet of courtly romance,
Henry van Veldeke, most of which was completed before 1174, that
French poetry of chivalry and romance had made an early and deep
impression in the Netherlands; and from the earliest surviving prose,
notably Beatrice of Nazareth's* Seven Manners of Loving, *it is
clear that such mastery of prose as they display can only be explained
by presupposing an intensive education, of women as well as men, in
the Latin Scriptures and classics of the spiritual life, and an already
flourishing tradition of lucid and flowing composition in the vernacular.*

*Beatrice and Hadewijch are the outstanding figures in the history
of the evolution in the Netherlands of the* Frauenbewegung, *that
great and victorious revolt of pious women, everywhere in Europe,
against the reactionary traditions which would have condemned them
in the cloisters as well as in the world to a role of subordination and
silence, which would have withheld from them the benefits of literacy*

and learning, which would have denied to them any active part in the great spiritual revivals and innovations which today we associate chiefly with the names of St Dominic and St Francis, but to which others, notably St Bernard, contributed as much. This 'women's movement' has been faithfully and brilliantly chronicled in recent years for the Rhineland and Germany by Herbert Grundmann; and in his fundamental work on the origins and the spread of the Beguines in the Low Countries, Alcantara Mens has depicted how there, as nowhere else in Europe, the newly-emancipated women religious were able to evolve a way of life hitherto unknown in the West, free from monastic enclosure, observing rules which they themselves devised to meet the needs of individual communities, following lives of intense activity which might be devoted to prayer, to teaching and study, to charitable works, or to all three.

Beatrice of Nazareth, in Seven Manners, tells us nothing of herself. For such information we have to go to a very few sources, notably Chrysostom Henriquez's Quinque Prudentes Virgines; and there we learn that she must have been born very soon after 1200, and that at the age of eleven she was sent to a house of Beguines at Zoutleeuw. The chronicle suggests that her family sent her there in the first place for education; but she was to live the rest of her life (she died in 1268) in such religious communities; and it is plain that she was enabled to cultivate to the full her great literary gifts. Judged solely on its artistic merits, Seven Manners is a great achievement, and her mellifluous fluency must surely have served in the next century as one of the models for the great Ruysbroek. She has been strongly influenced, as he too was to be, by St Bernard, the Victorines of Paris and by William of St-Thierry; and already she shows preoccupation with those teachings and ideas which we associate with Ruysbroek, with Tauler and with Eckhart: that searching of the soul for God which will lead it towards a union with Him so close 'that the soul no longer can perceive difference between itself and God', a union in which it will experience annihilation, a union from which it will return to find the earth a dessert and human existence a torment.

Though it is probable that Beatrice knew nothing of the Low German writings of her near-contemporary Mechtild of Magdeburg, their thought and their language are sometimes startlingly close. 'And like the fish, swimming in the vast sea and resting in its deeps, and like the bird, boldly mounting high in the sky, so the soul feels its spirit freely moving through the vastness and the depth and the unutterable richnesses of love' ... so Beatrice writes, inspired no doubt by St Paul; and in one of her prose poems Mechtild says that just as the fish must seek its natural home, the sea, and the bird find its freedom in the sky, so too must her soul find God.

To modern readers, not accustomed or sympathetic to the forms of medieval spirituality, there will no doubt be much in Beatrice which is distasteful if not repellant. Nourished as so many of us have been on the popular conception that religion should express itself in practical works, we may ask: 'What good did she do?' The next Netherlands writer to appear in this anthology, Hadewijch, is obviously conscious that such criticism could be levelled at such Beguines as Beatrice and herself; yet the answers which she provides will hardly be more satisfactory to the modern sceptic. Though she will often betray impatience with the religiosity of religious, as in Letter IV, and though she is convinced of the essentially apostolic and evangelical character of the contemplative vocation, as, of course, her own work witnesses, all of the Letters being in the form of instructions to a young Beguine, she is firm that the proper work of the contemplative is prayer and contemplation and nothing else. She and those like her have a duty to the world and especially to fallen sinners, but that duty consists only in intercession. To do more than that is what she calls 'needless involvement', and such work, she is very positive, is not for them: though what she does not say here but seems to imply is that there are others, notably priests, whose proper work the pastoral care of the fallen is, and who can do it better.

The soul's true work, for Hadewijch, is deificatio, striving for union with God; and she too resembles Mechtild of Magdeburg, in that she tells us more of the sorrows and torments of the soul in this

9

strife than of its joys and consolations. Doubtless she knew the famous passage in Hugh of St Victor, destined to be quoted and borrowed by countless spiritual writers, about 'the play of love', the ceaseless alternation of delight and pain for those who seek for God,

She uses the same metaphor when she writes, at the end of Letter I: 'In the beginning my sorrows were great enough, and I longed greatly for what I could not reach; but now it is as if someone were making sport of me, offering me something, and then, as I stretch out my hand, knocking it away and saying, "Wouldn't you like it?" and taking back again.' And in this same first letter she is playing on the concept of the love between God and the soul not as rest and peace and fulfilment, but contention and opposition and warfare as she says: 'God has been more angry with me than ever any devil was.' This may shock us, and doubtless it shocked those of her sisters who, she makes clear, opposed her teaching and her way of life, 'our false brethren who pretend that they dwell with us in the one house of the Faith', but we need not be scandalized if we will understand how profoundly her thought has been influenced, and how her language reflects the philosophy and the literary forms of courtly love, of Minne.

Mention has already been made of Henry of Veldeke, and recently Theodor Weevers has reminded us in his admirable account of the beginnings of medieval Dutch poetry that Henry was higly praised by the German poets whom we regard as the masters of the craft of singing the songs of courtly love, Wolfram of Eschenbach and Gottfried of Strasbourg among them, who called him their master and themselves his humble scholars. And in such spiritual writers as Hadewijch we have further testimony that before the fourteenth century, when there appeared that strong reaction in the Netherlands, notably expressed by Jacob of Maerlant, against the poetry of courtly love as blasphemous Venus-worship with which no god-fearing man should have to do, the analogies between the Christian's love of God and the humble, patient, unrewarded, penitential service, which Minne demanded of those whom she has enslaved, had been perceived and assimilated so completely that no discord or paradox was seen.

To say this is, of course, to beg many questions. No one has yet fully explored this field, to show us how much the concepts of courtly love, once they had found their way into the Mediterranean lands from the philosophers and poets of medieval Islam, became enriched and fertilized by Christian ideas and Christian devotion. We must be less prepared today than was, for example, Gilson a generation ago to assert that all the borrowing was by devout Christians from the neo-Ovidians who exploited these newfangled pagan notions as an act of rebellion against the Church's thinking and authority. None the less, in such a case as Hadewijch it is sufficiently evident that the analogy is something of this nature: I am bound to the service of the love of God just as any earthly knight knowingly and willingly enslaves himself to the service of that ideal love which is embodied in his lady. She will reward him or prolong his servitude and sufferings, as seems good to her, and he must always be her faithful servant, to death, in sorrow as in joy, as so must I with God. It is only the base peasant who thinks that the longings of love merit a prompt satisfaction; and if I demand from God happiness and consolation as the return here on earth for my service in His love, I too should be base, peasant-like, a villein *knowing nothing of* fine amour. *So Hadewijch says, in Letter VIII, of those lovers of God who are filled with fear: 'They long to suffer for Love, and so they learn all the fine usages of Love, for fear lest their words should be too churlish to reach the ears of Love.'*

Yet none of this is for her mere empty fashionable talk. In the first place her whole system of a Christianized Minne *is based on an accurate knowledge of human psychology, so that she can nonchalantly observe, for example: 'It is a sign of love that the beloved's name is sweet.' And she displays the practicality of her erudition when she at once links this with St Bernard's teaching on devotion to the Holy Name; and always she exhibits a down-to-earth sense in her approach to the idea that God is loved as* Minne *is served in courts and palaces: 'We all want to be God along with God; but God knows that there are few of us who want to be man with Him in His humanity, to carry*

His Cross with Him, to hang upon it with Him, to pay with Him the debt of human kind.'

It is needless here to multiply examples of Hadewijch's justness of touch, of that shrewdness and good feeling which holds her back from the excesses of *Brauttheologie*, from those analogies between divine and human love which less balanced readers and followers of St Bernard were so to exploit. Each one of the twenty (about half of the total) of her Letters here translated will reveal some different facet of her personality; and perhaps the most difficult and yet the finest of them all will be thought to be her Letter XVII, the careful, patient exposition of her mysterious and intricate poem, 'Seek after every virtue with a gracious zeal.' When, at the end of this letter, she tells us that in a moment of illumination she 'understood God's being.... Still I can find no language for what I have said,' is she telling us that this revelation came to her, not as a vision seen with spiritual eyes, but as a poem heard with spiritual ears, which she has kept in her memory and come little by little to know the true meaning of? To many readers, no doubt, resemblances will suggest themselves between this strange document and, on the one hand, Julian of Norwich's Revelations, on the other hand Rilke's Duino Elegies.

With Ruysbroek's Book of the Sparkling Stone we come to the second generation, as it were, of the Dutch mystical writers. The fervours of the thirteenth century, and the great numbers of female ecstatics, had produced much piety and devotion, but we cannot doubt that it also helped to encourage the many heretics who lived and taught in the Netherlands, of whom we remember chiefly the Brethren of the Free Spirit and their mysterious leader, the Brussels prophetess 'Bloemardinne'. (There was at one time a theory, first put out in the fifteenth century by Pomerius, that 'Bloemardinne' was a pseudonym of Hadewijch, but this was rank injustice to one of the very greatest of medieval European spiritual writers, who could only permit herself her extravagances of language and thought because she was fortified in her unimpeachable orthodoxy; and no one today would seriously advance this theory.) We know little of Bloemardinne and her wri-

tings, except by implication: Ruysbroek, already a middle-aged man who had served Ste Gudule in Brussels for many years of holy obscurity, first entered public life when he undertook a great and, it would seem, successful preaching campaign against her; and when, soon after, he retired to the 'desert' of Groenendael where in 1351 he took religious vows and founded a house of Augustinian canons and began to write, his earliest works, notably The Spiritual Espousals, *are deeply concerned with contrasting false mysticism with true. It was an English contemporary of his who called heretics 'the devil's contemplatives', and this is a dominant theme in many of Ruysbroek's treatises. The* Sparkling Stone *is, however, a later work, in which he is leass concerned to combat Manichaean Dualism, less anxious to rebut quietism and pantheism, than to teach, positively, how men who are called to that extraordinary way can attain to that union with God which he calls, in the* Espousals, *'living and fruitful.' This is not the place to write of the refinements of his doctrine or of his debt to his many great predecessors, from St Paul, St Augustine and 'pseudo-Dionysius' down to Hadewijch, whom he greatly reverenced; the best that one can do here is to commend the* Sparkling Stone *as one of the very finest pieces of affective writing to appear in the literature of Christian mysticism.*

It is not without interest that The Book of the Sparkling Stone *was known in late medieval England, in an English translation of the Latin version made by William Jordaens, under its alternative title,* The Treatise of Perfection of the Sons of God; *and the last works in this anthology have also contributed before now to English knowledge of Netherlands literature.* Mary of Nijmeghen, *translated not in its original dramatic form but as a prose narrative, was printed in Antwerp in the early sixteenth century, for export to England, by John Doesborgh, who had presses both there and in London, and the translator may have been one Laurence Andrews, who did such work for him. And in the 1920s Max Reinhardt used Maurice Maeterlinck's version of* Beatrice *as the scenario for his theatrical spectacle,* The Miracle, *which created such a sensation in New York and London.*

Beatrice *is preserved for us in a manuscript, now in the Royal Library at The Hague, which can be dated c. 1375. The poem itself is probably of the fourteenth century, but it is derived partly from a pious legend narrated by Caesarius of Heisterbach in the early thirteenth century, and there are many other parallels and analogues.*

We may today find the beginnings of Beatrice *perfunctory and crude, with singularly little attempt to explore what would, for the twentieth century, be the most interesting aspect of the story, the conflict in the nun's mind before she decided to break her vows. Partly this is because the poet can make his effect by a very perfunctory appeal to the conventions understood and accepted by his audience: Beatrice was enslaved by* Minne, *and once she had been pierced by the dart of Love, there was no help for her; and, he naively adds, 'We must not blame this nun, who was unable to escape from the love which held her captive, because the devil is always longing to tempt man....' But this somewhat scrambled opening is best accounted for as we read on and discover where the poet's real interests lie. As he warms to his central theme, that the vilest sinner must not despair of God's mercy, the whole temper of the poem changes, the artificiality and the conventions fall away, and the story moves easily and compellingly to its climax. Easily and compellingly, at least, for those who still share the conviction of the poet, and of his age, that man's greatest treasure is his immortal soul, which he imperils by mortal sin.*

The same conviction informs Mary of Nijmeghen *and the modern reader is as little helped as he is in* Beatrice *to understand the predicament in which the heroine finds herself. Why should a well-brought-up, decent, pious girl be so affected by her aunt's abuse that she calls upon the Devil? The aunt's rages and her miserable end we can believe in: she may be a stock figure, a 'humour' rather than a character, but she is drawn with such vigour and zest that she compels us to think that she is real; but Mary simply does not come alive until the moment when the play within the play strikes contrition into her heart. There is true drama and true pathos in the closing scenes, and when in answer to the Pope's horrified questions she says, 'Father, it was the good times, all the money and the presents which he gave me. . . ,' she is a forerunner of Gretchen, and speaks for all the poor foolish fallen girls in the world.*

More perhaps than any of the other works here, Mary of Nijmeghen *suffers and loses by translation. Whether or not it is the work of the Antwerp poetess Anna Bijns, it plainly was produced by one of her literary coterie, and the scenes at* The Golden Tree, *especially Emma-Mary's ballade in praise of rhetoric, have local and contemporary allusions which are lost on us today. The language of the original, too, with its exotic use of dialect and its constant crudity and obscenities, gives it an earthy strength which cannot be reproduced in English. It is only as the play reaches its climax that its appeal widens and becomes universal, so that we feel that we have in it one of the masterpieces of a great age.*

Beatrice of Nazareth

THERE ARE SEVEN MANNERS OF LOVING

There are seven manners of loving, which come down from the heights and go back again far above.

WALTHAM FOREST PUBLIC LIBRARIES

[I]

The first manner is an active longing, which proceeds from love, and must rule a long time in the heart before it can conquer all opposition, and can work with its power and judgment, and grow within us in holiness.

This manner is a longing which without doubt comes from love: that is, the pious soul, which faithfully wants to serve our Lord and to follow Him in holiness and truly to love Him, as it longs does everything in its power to attain and to keep the purity and the nobility and the freedom in which it was made by its Creator, in His image and likeness, which the soul must love greatly and zealously preserve. And the soul longs to lead its whole life so, and to act so and to grow and to climb to still greater heights of love and nearer knowledge of God, to that perfection for which it was made and is called by its Creator. This is all the soul's work, early and late, and to this the soul gives itself wholly. All the soul's seeking, all its teaching, all its petitions to God and all its meditations are for this: how it can approach and how it can attain to the presence and the likeness of love, adorned with all virtues and with that purity which is the sovereign excellence of love.

Always such a soul ponders what it is and what it ought to be, what it possesses and what it lacks; with its whole attention and with great longing and with all its powers it strives to preserve itself and to shun everything which could burden or hinder it as it works to this end. Its heart never ceases, its will never falters in seeking, entreating, learning, gaining and keeping everything which can help it and bring it to love.

This is the soul's greatest concern, when it is established in this way and can work so and labour greatly, until it is granted by

19

God, through its zeal and its faith, that it may thenceforth be in the service of love, no longer hindered by its past misdeeds, its conscience free and its spirit pure and its understanding clear.

Longing of this kind, of so great a purity and excellence, undoubtedly comes from love and not from fear. Fear makes us work and suffer, act and be still out of dread of the anger of our Lord, of the judgment of our righteous Judge, of punishment in eternity or of chastizing in this life. But love, in all that it does, strives for the purity and the exaltation and the supreme excellence which is love's very nature and possession and delight; and it is this striving which love teaches to those who serve love.

[2]

Yet the soul has a second manner of loving, when at times it offers itself to our Lord to serve Him for nothing, doing this only in love and asking for no answer, no reward of grace or of glory; but the soul is like a maiden who serves her master only for her great love of him, not for any payment, satisfied that she may serve him and that he suffers her to serve. So the soul longs to serve love with love, without measure, beyond measure, and beyond human sense and reason, faithfully performing every service.

When the soul attains this state, it becomes so ardent in longing, so ready to serve, so joyful labouring, so calm in sorrow, so gay in suffering; and with every quality which it possesses the soul longs to be pleasing to its love, and all that it asks is to act and to suffer for the use and the honour of love.

[3]

The third manner of loving is attained by the pious soul when it comes into a time of much suffering. This is when the soul longs to be sufficient for love, to perfect itself for the honour of love and to serve it in every way, in utter obedience and submission.

Sometimes this desire grows violent in the soul, and it is seized with great longings to perform all things and to achieve all virtues, to suffer and to endure everything, to make all its works perfect in love, withholding nothing and counting nothing. In this state the soul is ready to do anything, eager and unafraid in labours and in suffering; and yet in all that it does the soul remains unfulfilled and dissatisfied.

But it is above all else the greatest torment to the soul that despite its great longings it cannot do enough for love, and that in loving it comes so short. Yet it knows well that it is above human ability and beyond its powers to do as it wishes, for what it longs to do is impossible and unnatural to created beings. For the soul longs single-handed to do as much as all the men upon earth, as all the spirits in heaven, as every creature that ever is, to do more beyond all telling than they do, serving, loving, glorifying love as is love's due. And because the soul comes so short in what it does, it wants with all its will and with great longing to do yet better. Yet this cannot satisfy the soul. It knows well that to achieve what it longs for is far above its powers, beyond human reason and all the senses; yet it cannot moderate or restrain or calm itself. It does everything that it can; it gives thanks and praises to love; it acts and it works for love, it surrenders its whole self for love, and all its works are perfected for love.

But none of this gives the soul any rest, and it is a great torment to long for what it cannot attain. And so the soul must stay in sorrow and longing, and it will seem that living, it dies, and dying, it feels the pains of hell, and its whole life is torment and rejection and refusal, racked as it is with these desires which it can never appease or quieten or satisfy. And the soul must remain in this anguish till the time when our Lord comforts it and establishes it in a different manner of loving and longing, when He gives it a closer knowledge of Himself; and then the soul can do as our Lord allows it.

[4]

In the fourth manner of loving, it is our Lord's custom to give sometimes great joy, sometimes great woe; and let us now speak of this.

Sometimes it happens that love is sweetly awakened in the soul and joyfully arises and stirs itself in the heart without any help from human acts. And then the heart is so tenderly touched in love, so powerfully assailed, so wholly encompassed and so lovingly embraced in love that the soul is altogether conquered by love. Then it feels a great closeness to God and a spiritual brightness and a wonderful richness and a noble freedom and a great compulsion of violent love, and an overflowing fullness of great delight. And then the soul feels that all its senses and its will have become love, that it has sunk down so deeply and been engulfed so completely in love, that it has itself entirely become love. Love's beauty has adorned the soul, love's power has consumed it, love's sweetness has submerged it, love's righteousness has engulfed it, love's excellence has embraced it, love's purity has enhanced it, love's exaltedness has drawn it up and enclosed it, so that the soul must be nothing else but love and do nothing else.

When the soul feels itself to be thus filled full of riches and in such fullness of heart, the spirit sinks away down into love, the body seems to pass away, the heart to melt, every faculty to fail; and the soul is so utterly conquered by love that often it cannot support itself, often the limbs and the senses lose their powers. And just as a vessel filled up to the brim will run over and spill if it is touched, so at times the soul is so touched and overpowered by this great fullness of the heart that in spite of itself it spills and overflows.

In the fifth manner, it also sometimes happens that love is powerfully strengthened in the soul and rises violently up, with great tumult and force, as if it would break the heart with its assault and drag the soul out of itself in the exercise and the delight of love. And then the soul is drawn in the longing of love to fulfill the great and pure deeds of love and the desires implanted by love's many promptings. Or sometimes the soul longs to rest in the sweet embrace of love, in that desirable state of richness and satisfaction which comes from the possession of love, so that the heart and all the senses long and seek eagerly and long wholly for this. When the soul is in this state, it is so strong in spirit, so open in heart to receive all things, so stronger in bodily power to do all things, more able to accomplish its works, achieving so much, that it seems to the soul itself that there is nothing which it cannot do and perform, even though in the body it were to remain idle. At the same time the soul feels itself so greatly stirred from within, such an utter dependence upon love, such an impatient desire for love and the countless sorrows of a deep dissatisfaction. And sometimes when the soul experiences love that brings it woe without it ever knowing why, or it may be because it is so stirred to long for love, or because it is filled with dissatisfaction that it cannot know love's full delight.

And at times love becomes so boundless and so overflowing in the soul, when it itself is so mightily and violently moved in the heart, that it seems to the soul that the heart is wounded again and again, and that these wounds increase every day in bitter pain and in fresh intensity. It seems to the soul that the veins are bursting, the blood spilling, the marrow withering, the bones softening, the heart burning, the throat parching, so that the body in its every part feels this inward heat, and this is the fever of love. Sometimes the soul feels that the whole body is transfixed, and it is as if every sense would fail; and like a devouring fire, seizing upon everything and consuming everything which it can master, love seems to be working violently in the soul, relentless, uncontrollable, drawing everything into it and devouring it.

All this torments and afflicts the soul, and the heart grows sick and the powers dwindle; yet it is so that the soul is fed and love is fostered and the spirit is subjected to love.

For love is exalted so high above the soul's comprehension, above all that the soul can do or suffer, that even though at such times it may long to break the bond that unites it to love, that cannot harm love's singleness; and the soul is so fettered with the bond of love, so conquered by the boundlessness of love, that it cannot rule itself by reason, cannot reason through understanding, cannot spare itself this weariness, cannot hold fast to human wisdom.

For the more there is given from above to the soul, the more is demanded of it: the more is revealed to the soul, the more it is filled with longing to come close to the light of that truth, that purity, that excellence and that delight which are love's attributes. Always the soul will be driven and goaded on, never will it be satisfied and at rest. For what most afflicts and torments the soul is that which most heals and assuages it; what gives the soul its deepest wounds brings to it best relief.

[6]

In the sixth manner, as the bride of our Lord advances and climbs into greater holiness, she feels love to be of a different nature, and her knowledge of this love is closer and higher.

The soul feels that love has conquered its every shortcoming, and has mastered the senses and adorned its humanity, and increased and exalted its being, and has utterly overpowered it without any resistance, so that the heart is made steadfast in confidence, and can freely practise all the exercises of love and delight in love and take its rest. When the soul is in this state, there is nothing which it must perform or abandon, suffer and endure, which does not seem to it petty and easy, for this is one of love's noble qualities, and so it is easy for the soul to busy itself in the exercises of love.

Then the soul feels in itself a closeness to God which comes from Him, a radiant purity, a sweetness of the spirit, a loving freedom, a savouring wisdom, a gentle drawing near to our Lord and a close comprehension of God.

And you may see that now the soul is like a housewife who has put all her household in good order and prudently arranged it and well disposed it: she has taken good care that nothing will damage it, her provision for the future is wise, she knows exactly what she is doing, she acquires and discards, she does what is proper, she avoids mistakes, and always she knows how everything should be. So it is with the soul: the soul is all love, and love rules in the soul, mighty and powerful, working and resting, doing and not doing, and all which is in the soul and comes to the soul is according to love's will.

And like the fish, swimming in the vast sea and resting in its deeps, and like the bird, boldly mounting high in the sky, so the soul feels its spirit freely moving through the vastness and the depth and the unutterable richnesses of love.

It is love's power which has seized the soul and led it, sheltered and protected it, given it prudence and wisdom and the sweetness and the strength which belong to love. Yet still at this time love hides from the soul its own power, that it has mounted to yet greater heights and that it is master of itself and that it is love which reigns triumphantly in it. And then love makes the soul so bold that it no longer fears man nor friend, angel or saint or God Himself in all that it does or abandons, in all its working and resting. And now the soul feels indeed that love is within it, as mighty and as active when the body is at rest as when it performs many deeds.

The soul knows well and feels that love is not found in the labours and the sufferings of those in whom it rules, but that all who want to attain to love must seek it in fear and pursue it in faith, exercising themselves in longing, not sparing themselves in great labours, in many sufferings, undergoing many sorrows and enduring much contempt. The soul must not despise these things: small though they be, they must seem great, until it attains to the state where love rules in it and performs its own mighty works, making great things small, labour easy, suffering sweet, and all debts paid.

This is freedom of conscience, sweetness of heart, subjection of the senses, the soul's excellence, the spirit's exaltation, and the beginning of everlasting life. This is to live the life of angels here in the flesh, that everlasting life which may God grant to us all. Amen.

[7]

Yet the blessed soul has a seventh manner of yet higher loving, in which it will experience little activity of itself. For it is drawn, above humanity, into love, and above human sense and reason and above all the works of the heart, and it is drawn along with love alone into eternity and incomprehensibility, into the vastness and the unattainable exaltation and into the limitless abyss of Divinity, which is all in all things, remaining incomprehensible in all things, immutable in all being, all-powerful, all-comprehending, all-doing in its might.

And in this the blessed soul sinks down so deeply and softly in love, it is so mightly led in desire, that the heart fails and is within full of disquiet, the soul flows away and liquefies in love, the spirit is possessed with the violence of great longing. All the senses prompt the soul to long for the delight of love. The soul begs and entreats this from God, it seeks it ardently in God, it cannot but long for it above all, for love will not allow the soul to dally or find rest or be at peace. Love draws it on, love thrusts it back, love gives it death and brings it life, love heals it and then wounds it again, love makes it sorry and then glad again: and so love draws the soul on up into a higher life.

So the soul has climbed in spirit above time into eternity, it is exalted above all that love can give into the eternity which is love itself, which is beyond time, which is set above all human modes of love, the soul has transcended its own nature in its longing for the life which is there.

Its life and its longing, its desires and its love are all there in that unshakeable truth and that pure brightness, that noble exaltation and that transfiguring beauty, in the sweet company of those highest spirits who all flow out in the superabundance of love, who have their being in the bright knowledge, the possession and the delight of their love. The will of the soul is set up there among those spirits: it is there that it longs to be, and most of all among the flaming seraphim; and whilst still here in the body it finds its rest and its dearest dwelling-place in the immense Divinity, in the exalted Trinity.

The soul seeks God in His majesty, it finds Him there and it beholds Him with heart and with spirit. It knows Him, it loves Him, it longs for Him, so much that it cannot heed saints or angels, men or created things, except in that common love which it has towards Him in whom it loves all. It is He alone whom the soul has chosen in love, above all, beneath all, in all, so that with all the longing of its heart and all the strength of its spirit it longs to see Him and to have Him and to delight in Him.

And now this earth is for the soul a cruel exile and a dire prison and a heavy torment: it despises the world, the earth revolts it, and here is nothing earthly which can console or satisfy it, and it is for the soul a great punishment that it must live in this estrangement and appear so alien. It cannot forget that it is in exile, its longings cannot be stilled, its desires torment it so cruelly and it is so martyred and afflicted that it is beyond all measure and without any measure.

Therefore the soul is filled with great longing te be set free from this exile, to be loosed from this body; and sometimes it says with sorrowing heart, as the apostle said: *Cupio dissolvi et esse cum Christo*, that is 'I long to be set free and to be with Christ.' So it longs greatly and with a tormenting impatience for death to this world and for life with Christ; and this is not because the soul abhors this present time or fears the afflictions which time may bring, but because a holy and eternal love makes it to desire, in longing and languishing and great coveting, to attain to the land of eternity and into the glories of love's delight.

This longing is so great and violent in the soul, this present life is to it so hard and cruel, that the torments which it suffers in its longings cannot be described. Yet the soul must live in hope, and it is hope which makes it yearn and pine. Oh, holy longings of love, how mighty you are in the loving soul! This is a blessed martyrdom, a cruel suffering, a long torment, a murderous death and an expiring life. The soul cannot gain the heights above, nor can it rest or stay here below. To think of God is longing such as it cannot endure, to lack Him fills it with tormenting longing. And so the soul must go on living in great sorrow.

And therefore the soul cannot, will not be consoled, as the prophet says: *Renuit consolari anima mea*, 'My soul refuses to be comforted.' So the soul refuses every consolation, often from God Himself and from His creatures, for every consolation which could come to it only strengthens its love and draws it up towards a higher life; and this renews the soul's longing to live in love and to delight in love, its determination to live unconsoled in this present exile. And so there is no gift which can appease or comfort it, for the soul's one need is to be in the presence of its love.

This is a hard and laborious life, for the soul will take no consolation here, but longs only to achieve what it seeks so restlessly. Love has seized it and led it and taught it to walk love's ways, and the soul has followed them so faithfully, sometimes in great labour and in painful works, in great longings and in cruel desires, in much impatience and in woeful displeasure, in joy and in sorrow and in much suffering, in seeking and searching, in wanting and having, in climbing and in drawing back, in following and pursuing, in need and in pain, in fear and sorrow, in woe and desolation, in great faith and in much doubt. The soul is ready to suffer in well and in woe, in death and in life it wishes to belong to love, and in its heart it feels the suffering of cruel pain, and for the sake of love it longs to come to its true home. And when the soul has known all this, all it desires is to flee from earth to heaven; for all the works of love are ruled by the soul's longing to live close to love, its striving to ascend to love, where it can be nearest to love.

So the soul always wishes to follow after love, to see love, to delight in love; and this cannot come to the soul here in this exile. So it longs to leave this life and find its home, where already it has established its dwelling, where it directs its longings that it may in love find rest. For the soul knows well that there all hindrances will be removed, that there it will in love by its own true love be received.

For there the soul will look upon that which it has so sorrowfully longed for: it will have Him for its eternal reward whom it has so faithfully served, and find the delight of every consolation in Him whom so often it has in love embraced in the soul.

Then it will enter into the joy of its Lord, as St Augustine says: 'Who goes into the joy of the Lord goes into Him, and he shall not fear, for in Him who is perfect shall all perfection be had.'

There the soul will be united with its Bridegroom, and will become with Him one spirit in an indivisible love and in everlasting faith. And the soul which has striven in the time of grace shall rejoice in Him in everlasting glory, where all our work will be to praise and love Him.

May God make speed to bring us all to this. Amen.

Hadewijch of Antwerp

LETTERS

God, who by His life of virtues illumined the bright love that had been uncomprehended, when in the light of His love He gave light to every virtuous life, may He enlighten and illumine you with that shining light in which He Himself is illumined, and all His friends and those whom He most dearly loves.

The greatest light which men can have upon earth is truth in works of righteousness, done here and now, and to serve truth above all forms of being, for love of the light of that noble love which is God. Ah, how bright is that light, when we let God work His will with His light! For when we do this, love brings itself to be, and all creatures, each one according to his fashion, ordained for him by God in His goodness, are brought to be, performing works of righteousness in this light.

Therefore, I ask you, as a friend to his dear friend, and I entreat you, as a sister to her dear sister, and I bid you, as a mother to her dear child, and I command you in your love, as a bridegroom commands his beloved bride, that you open the eyes of your heart wide to the light, and that you see and reverence yourself in God.

Learn to behold what God is: how here in this present life He is the truth of all things, and how He flows through all His rich gifts, He their only goodness, and how He is altogether the sum of all virtues, He for whose sake in heaven they sing a threefold *Sanctus;* for His three names, each in its own being, contain all virtues and present them through the three beings.

See how like a father God has protected you, and what He has given you, and what He has promised you. See how great these loves are, one towards the other, and by your love give thanks to Him, which you do if you see that this is God, and if you work in Him by His light, delighting in His glory and manifesting all things in His clarity, that each thing may be illumined or overshadowed as its nature may be.

For the sake of all this, which is God, for its sake we must allow God to have joy in Himself, in His works which partake of His light—*sicut in celo et in terra*—and we must ever say, with our words and with our works, *fiat voluntas tua*.

Ah, dear child, the more His vast power is illumined in you, and the better His holy will is performed in you, and the more His shining truth is bright in you, the more must you long to forgo all consolations and repose, so that you may attain to God's great all. Illumine your being, adorn yourself with virtues and with works of righteousness, throw open wide your senses, longing intensely with each of them for the all which is God. And order your soul that it may come to have great delight in the all-powerful love of God, whose sweetness we may not well sustain.

Ah, dear child, though I talk of an unbearable sweetness I have never, never known it, except only in the wish of my heart, and what I have endured for His love has been sweet to me. But He has been more angry with me than ever any devil was: for no devil was ever able to keep me from loving Him, nor did it ever please me to serve anyone but Him. But it is He who has taken Himself away from me. What He is, that He consumes in the sweetness of his joy, and He leaves me to lament thus, deprived of that delight, and He leaves me still so burdened down with my fruitless longings for His love, and He leaves me joyless of all the joys that should replenish me.

Ah me, alas that He should tell me of His true love and send me pledges of His joys, and should now let it all pass from me, as you yourself in part can see. God knows, I made Him my master in all things, and little did I ask of Him but that which was His own will; but that which He offered to me I would gladly have taken for my joy, had it been His will to bring me to it. In the beginning my sorrows were great enough, and I longed greatly for what I could not reach; but now it is as if someone were making sport of me, offering me something, and then, as I stretch out my hand, knocking it away and saying, "Wouldn't you like it?" and taking it back again.

Look now upon all the things for the sake of which you have gone astray through your own obstinacy, bringing needless sorrows upon yourself. Yet it is true, I know very well, that a man suffers cruelly who has wandered away from his true love, and one sees indeed that then he does not know whether he is near to Him or far off from Him. But the true believer will know that the goodness of Him whom he loves is greater than his own frailty. One must not sorrow because of one's labours, nor ought one to long for rest. One should renounce everything one has, for the sake of everything one wants, and deny oneself all rest. Always be joyful, believing in the love which you shall win. For if you have a perfect desire for the love of God, then no other kind of rest can content you except His love alone.

Be on your guard, and do not let your peace be disturbed by anything. Do everything well which you do, but do not trouble yourself with any thought of what you may obtain: not happiness, not damnation, not blessedness, not torment; but do everything, or let it alone, to the glory of Him whom you love. If you follow this rule, you will soon triumph. Let people think you a fool if they want: they may well be right. Be courteous and serviceable to all those who have need of you, and comply with every man's wishes when you may without lowering your standards. Rejoice with those who are joyful, lament with those who weep, and be compassionate towards those who need your pity. Tend the sick diligently, be pitiful to the needy, and in your spirit be at unity and free of all God's creatures. And so, as you do the best of which you are capable in all things, however frail human nature may be, have trust in the goodness of God, that His goodness is greater than your weakness. Do what you do trusting in him and with a virtuous intention, be devoted and constant, never ceasing to fulfil our Lord's precepts and to perform His dearest will in all things in which you can see it, labouring and scrutinizing your thoughts closely, so that you may know yourself for what you are.

And live so for God, this I ask of you, that you do not fall short in any of the great works to which He has called you: do not fail in any work, however small, this I ask and counsel you. There are many reasons why you should take upon you to labour for the love of God: for He has protected you from every occasion of sin, if you wanted to be protected, so that the good which you did was done by His grace, if you would confess it. And in all that you have done there has been little enough pain, and it is by pain that we grow; and grow we must if we are to serve God aright, and therefore sometimes be glad that you suffer.

But even if at times you feel in your heart that you are lost from God, as if He had deserted you, do not despair of yourself because of that. For I tell you truly that all the desolation which we suffer with a good will towards God is pleasing to Him in His whole nature. But it would not be profitable for us to know how acceptable this is to God, for if we did there would be no desolation for us, for if anyone could know that that were acceptable to the will of God, he would gladly and willingly be in the depths of hell, and then he could not advance and grow, because then he would feel no torment. The man who could know that what he did was pleasing to God would never care what became of him.

You are still young, you need to grow, and it will be better for you, if you want to advance along the way of love, to undertake labours and suffer for the honour of love, than to have rest and joy in love. But you must serve love as one who seeks no more than always to be in love's honourable bondage, and therefore you must not seek to avoid either the honours or the shames of love, not the torments of earth or of hell if by suffering them you may come to serve love worthily. Suffer worthily for love in saying your office, in keeping your rule, in all your obligations, neither wanting nor finding rest. And if you were to find rest in anything other than God Himself, Him in whom only your being ought to delight, wherever that rest might be found, you must not stay there, you must wait for the time when God's being shall send you light and give you strength to practise the usages of love and to delight in the being of love, there where love is filled and content with its own self.

Make your service of love a beautiful thing: want nothing else, fear nothing else, and let love be free to become what love truly is. Though love may tarry, when she comes she brings the richest gifts. Whatever your misgivings, whatever your misfortunes, never cease to perform the works of virtue. Nor should you be anxious in your misfortunes in case you shall never be restored to God. Never doubt this, never fear what men and saints and angels seem to say, not even when they seem to bring wonderful signs; for long ago you were called, and sometimes in your heart you feel that you are chosen, and that God now begins to support your spirit, and that you may have trust in His strength.

Give yourself up to this so perfectly that He may make you perfect. Never again seek for any man's help in heaven nor on earth, whatever his power may be, for, believe me, it is as I say: you are supported by God, and it must be your will to be supported by His great might, and no longer to hold back and doubt.

There is only one fear that we should always have: that we are too little to serve love as it deserves. This is a fear which fills a man with love, and because of it devotion seizes on him and overwhelms him. But should it seem to him that he has done enough for love, and that love does too little for him, not loving him as his honourable services deserve, then as long as he thinks so he is lacking in fear, reproaching love in this way with faithlessness. You must put away all other fears than this from you, and this fear you must open your heart to, and let it come and go as it will.

Suffer the anguish which God sends you, rejoice in it, cherish it;

and you will hear His secret counsels, as Job says of Him: 'To me a secret word has been spoken.'

There are two kinds of support which men may indeed give to one another. The first is when they help up sinners who have fallen. Those who do this are sometimes so pierced with love for their fellows that they are willing to forgo the joy and the blessedness which they might have in God, for the sake of sinners who are in a state of sin, so that they would rather be deprived of God themselves than fear that there are sinners who despair of His grace. In this way love makes one man to support another.

The second kind of support is when God sees that men are strong and firm in virtue and love; seeing that they are so mighty and so confident, He does not spare them suffering, so that well-being does not spoil them, the abundance of consolation does not make them complacent. They must always be prepared to lack everything which He could give them if that could bring sinners to Him. For there are some sinners of noble nature and great natural capacity, who have yet so ruined and destroyed themselves that unaided they might never win their way back to God. But still He is so gracious to them that He moves those men, whom He finds to be strong in themselves, to pity sinners, to help them for His sake, and to lead them back to the path of His true love.

This sort of help for sinners is not for you; for you began early, nor have you in your way of life ever disowned God, so that He shall indeed bring you to His life, if only you will entrust yourself to Him. But I will tell you how you can help: follow the promptings of your heart, living only in God. No one lives in God who is a stranger to Him: he whom you know or believe or feel to have his dwelling-place in God, who has been brought to God and has his conversation and his life steadfastly in God, he has mounted above you, and him you may follow and obey without abasing yourself.

If you wish to gain all these things, which are yours, for yourself, then you must in perfect confidence in God abandon all things, to become what He is; and for the honour of love, you must constantly deny yourself, so as to achieve a pure obedience in all things which are needful to the greatest perfection, whether they are works to be done or to be let alone. To this end you must preserve humility, not glorying in any work which you can do, and you must have the prudence of perfect love and charity, nurturing everything on earth and in heaven as true love would have you do it. If you have the will to it, you may thus become perfect and gain this for yourself.

LETTER 3

God be with you. I beg you, through that perfect virtue and faith which God Himself is, that you remember, every hour, the holy virtue which God Himself is, and which He was in all His ways when He lived upon this earth. Ah, my sweet love, now we too live upon earth. Think now of the noble works which He performed for the sake of all men, according to each one's needs, and think too of the sweet nature of the love which He now is, and which is yet so terrible and so wonderful to behold.

Ah, but wisdom leads us deep down into God. And since this is so, there is no other safe course in life than to seek only after this deep wisdom, and so to draw near to Him. And wisdom herself is so lost to us, so far from our searching, that He must sorrow that in this world there are so few who seek, who yearn impatiently, who strive with the ardent works of love to attain Him, His mysterious nature and His life of love. Here upon earth we might know much of the ways of heaven, if only we might withdraw ourselves from earthly ways, drawn by the bond of love, if we were filled with a heavenly longing for God and with a brotherly love for men in all things of which they are in need.

First I mention love's greatest need and love's first care: for so does that brotherly love which lives in the divine love of Jesus Christ; and it is His love which is the foundation of brotherly love, whatever its works may be, whether in joys or in sorrows, in power or in goodness, in serving or in counsel, in comfort or in admonition. Therefore let all your powers be directed towards Christ, give Him no cause to reproach you. If you come upon Him so, He has no defence against you; for to give Himself thus to you is the work of His being and the will of His Father, which His Father commanded and He has performed; and it is the message of the Holy Spirit. Then love shall make heavenly wonders known, and shall do many marvels.

LETTER 4

I ask this of you, that you should observe all the points where you have gone astray, and do all that is in your power to do better in such matters, for we go astray in only too many things which are good in themselves, and in which we mean to do well. Yet it is our reason which is at fault, because we neither understand nor seek after that which is best; and so reason errs. And then when the reason is not clear, the will is made feeble and powerless, and so men's labours are heavy, because they are not illumined by the reason. The memory forgets its sublime intentions, its supreme and joyful trust in God, and the many valiant resolutions which that trust formed in it that it would wait patiently here in this exile for Him whom it loves. In this way the noble soul becomes oppressed. Yet even so, its expectation of God's goodness comforts it; but one must suffer and labour before one's burden is lightened.

Now you must observe all the things which I shall say to you, and see where your reason has gone astray, and strive as hard as you can to improve; and do not be too grieved when you see your own shortcomings. For a humble, perfect knight will never sorrow for the blows which he has received, as he beholds the wounds of his holy champion. When it seems well to God, they shall at once be healed; till then, labour valiantly. For God shall give light and steadfastness and truth to the reason, and reason shall direct the will, and from that shall new strength come. And then the memory shall become sharp, as God in His great power takes from us every sort of fear and dread.

To be brief, the reason goes astray in fearing, in hoping, in loving, in keeping rules, in weeping, in yearning for devotion, in seeking for consolation, in dreading God's admonitions, in over-scrupulousness, in taking, in giving; in so many things which seem good to men reason goes astray.

Reason knows well that we must dread God, that God is great and man is little. But when reason fears the greatness of God, comparing it with our own littleness, thinking that such littleness has no claim upon such greatness, and begins to doubt if man can ever be the dearest child of God, thinking that His nature, which is so great, can take no account of man—this causes many to cease seeking for God in His greatness. Reason has gone astray in this, and in many other matters.

Many people err in their hope, believing that God has already forgiven them all their sins; if their sins were truly all forgiven them, they would love God and would perform the works of love, but in their hope they forsake these works and put their trust in things that cannot ever be of avail. For they are slothful and will not pay the great debt which they owe to God, and to His love which they should be willing to repay even with their very lives. In such false hope reason goes astray, and men thinking so err in many other matters; though there is less need of saying this to you than other things.

Men go astray in loving, when they give more than they should, when they are needlessly involved, when they do more than is required; in such ways a man afflicts himself to no purpose. Many are moved by mere affection, calling it a godly love.

When men keep rules, they burden themselves with many affairs of which they could well be free, and so their reason goes astray. There is a spirit of good will which can achieve more in our hearts than all the rules that anyone can invent.

In weeping men go much astray; for though reason may tell us that we weep for our failings, it is much more our self-will that grieves us, and in this many go most grievously astray.

All those men err who yearn for devotion because they seek in it for some thing; for they ought to seek for God and for nothing else; though what He gives in addition to Himself we should gladly accept.

In seeking for consolation men often err; for it is their own affections which they seek to gratify, be their love directed towards God or men.

The wrath of God and the many terrors which come from contemplating it cause reason to err, for the more men regard it the more they seek to distract themselves oftentimes with works, and because of that forsake love.

Over-scrupulousness, too much concern with what one should do and what one should avoid, robs love of much of its freedom.

When one accepts those things, for the body or the spirit, without which one could very well do, reason goes astray.

In possessions of many sorts, in unwarranted pleasure in them, in a too anxious hold upon one's peace with God and men, in these does reason err.

In giving men often err greatly; for they seek to offer up themselves entirely, before the time has come when they may be acceptable, and they wish to devote themselves to many alien things in which God is neither intended nor loved.

In remorse, in suffering, in rest, in anger, in reconciliation, in joys and in sorrows: when we devote our precious time to all these things, reason there goes astray.

A too much divided obedience makes reason grievously to err, and all these previous matters are included in this. It is self-will which makes us slavishly obedient to fear, immoderate in our obedience to all these other things. Such obedience to fear, to hope, to affection and to all to which we are subject is not a part of perfect love; and in this reason errs.

If I say that reason is led astray in all these matters which people generally approve, it is because they are all of great importance, and it is reason which should show us what their true importance is.

LETTER 5

God be with you who are so dear to my heart, and give you comfort and peace in Himself. Beyond all other things which I may wish you, may God uphold you with His peace, and comfort you with His own goodness, and illumine you with the splendour of His Spirit, as indeed He shall, and joyfully, if only you will have faith in Him and rely enough upon Him.

Ah, dear child, sink down with all your soul entirely into Him, and sink away from all those things which are no part of love, whatever may overwhelm you. We have much to endure, and if we can hold fast, so we shall grow to our full stature.

It is a great perfection to be able to suffer all things from all men; but, God knows, it is the greatest perfection of all to suffer at the hands of our false brethren, who pretend that they dwell with us in the one house of the faith. Ah, you need not wonder, though I sorrow for it, that those whom we chose out, to live with us a life of praises to Him whom we love, nowadays rail against us, and disturb our fellowship for the sake of keeping us apart, of keeping me from communion with anyone. And yet how inexpressibly sweet love shows itself to be to me, how sweet are the gifts which come to me from love! Ah, to love I can deny nothing; and you, can you wait patiently, can you hold out until that love comes which men say conquers everything?

Ah, my dear one, why has not love yet sufficiently subdued you, not drawn you down into its depths? Alas, since love is so sweet, why do you not cast yourself down into it and lose your-

43

self? Why do you not reach out into God, into the depths of His unfathomable nature? You whom I love, give yourself, for love's sake, wholly in love to God. You must do this, for as it is we both suffer: what you do makes you suffer, and I suffer greatly for you.

Ah, my dear love, do not grow weary of pursuing virtue, whatever your pains may be. You spend so much effort on so many things which are of little use to you. You waste so much time in your haste, rushing out to meet every little event; and I cannot persuade you to be more moderate. Whatever you want to do you fall upon as if your life depended on it. I am glad that you console and help those who are your friends, and the better you do it the gladder I shall be; so long as you and they preserve peace of heart, I shall be glad.

I ask you and I warn you, in that perfect faith which love is, to do or to leave alone all that I have bidden you; and since we know sorrows that are inconsolable, console the sorrowful as best you can. And above all I command you to keep every letter of that law of love which has been laid upon us, holding yourself untouched by any of this world's sorrows and regrets.

LETTER 6

Now I want to warn you about one thing from which great harm can come. I assure you that this is one of the worst sicknesses which prevail today, and sicknesses there are in plenty. Nowadays everyone is constantly questioning the good faith of his friends, putting them to the test and complaining of their faithlessness; and people spend their time in this way who ought to be filled with an exalted love for our great God.

What does it matter to us, if our intention is good and we want to exalt our lives to God, who is so great and so exalted, whether people are faithful or unfaithful to us, kind or unkind, treat us ill or well? If we cannot show good faith and kindness to them,

44

we are harming ourselves, and the worst of the harm is that we are ruining for ourselves the sweetness of true love.

If anyone keeps good faith with you and consoles you in your need with his help, you must show your gratitude and help him in his turn, but, more than this, we must serve and love God the more fervently because of this, and leave it to Him to reward others or not as He wills. For He in His being is just, and when He gives or takes away it is always justly done; for He is exalted in the delight of His own being, and we are here, infinitely beneath Him in all our shortcomings. And especially you and I, who have not yet attained what we are, not yet acquired what we have, fall so far short of what is ours, we must forgo everything if we are to be and to have everything, we must learn, in the unity and boldness of the spirit learn the perfect life of that love which has moved us both to its works.

Ah, dear child, above all I beg you to be on your guard against instability. For there is nothing so able and so quick to separate you from our Lord as instability. Whatever troubles may come to you, do not commit the folly of believing that you are set for any other goal than the great God Himself, in the fullness of His being and of His love; do not let folly or doubt deflect you from any good practice which can lead you to this goal. If you will confide yourself to His love, you will soon grow to your full stature, but if you persist in doubting, you will become sluggish and grudging, and everything which you ought to do will be a burden to you. Let nothing trouble you, do not believe that anything which you must do for Him whom you seek will be beyond your strength, that you cannot surmount it, that it will be beyond you. This is the fervour, this is the zeal which you must have, and all the time your strength must grow.

And when you find any man who hungers for God's love, who labours for it, who lives in exile wanting it and suffers many pains for it, do all you can to help such a one, hold nothing back from him: give him your heart in compassionate affection, your

45

counsel in consolation, your labours in service and toil. Towards sinners show compassion, and pray many prayers for them to God. But beyond saying prayers for them, and fervently asking God to free them from their sins, have nothing to do with them: you would be wasting your time and achieving very little.

But those who do love God you must requite with love, helping to strengthen them so that their love for Him may grow. That you must do for them, and nothing more. And for those weaker ones, sinners separated from God, great labours and special prayers are not required from you: merely include them in your love for God. The more God's lovers love Him, the more are sinners set free from their sins, the more are His lovers confirmed in their love.

To live in perfect accord with the will of His love is to live so wholly in that will of that true love, longing always to be all that love asks of us, that even if we wished we would choose and ask nothing better than what pleases love, whether the world should curse us or bless us for it. Nor should we ever wish the peace and the blessedness of that love to fail in us, except only so that we may know that we are not yet grown to the perfect stature of love.

And knowing this we must always know that for us life must be a loving service and a longing exile, for so Jesus Christ lived as a man upon this earth. It is nowhere written that Christ in all His earthly life ever asked for any privilege from His Father or from His own omnipotent nature, so that He might here enjoy the blessedness of His divine being; He never granted Himself any respite, but lived in greater toil from day to day, from His first day until His last. It was His gracious will to live as we must live, to be what we should be, and He says to those who live now as He then did that where there is love there is great labour and much suffering. But to such men, their sufferings are sweet. *Qui amat non laborat*, 'Who loves does not labour.'

When Christ lived here as man, there was a time for all His

works. When the proper time came, He did the proper work: His words and His deeds, His preaching and teaching, His admonitions, consolations, miracles, absolutions, His toils, His reproofs, His humiliations, His griefs, His sorrows until His Passion and death: in all these He waited patiently for the right time. And when the hour came for Him to work, He perfected it, valiant and mighty, and in these great and honest labours He paid the debt which every human being owes to the Father, who is God and who is truth. 'Mercy and truth met one another, justice and peace embraced one another.'

In union with God's humanity, you should live here in labour and exile; and in union with God's eternal omnipotence you should in your heart love and rejoice, gently laying all your trust in Him. In the truth which that humanity and that omnipotence share, God finds a single delight; and just as His humanity here on earth submitted to the will of His majesty, you too must submit in love to the will of Them both together. Humbly serve Them, in Their united might, and stand before Them as one standing ready to do all Their will. And let Them then do with you what They will.

Let this be your only concern, and nothing else. Serve God's majesty with ready hands, and with a great desire for every work of virtue. You should love God's divinity not merely with devotion but with unspeakable longings, standing always with renewed fervour before Him as He manifests Himself, dreadful in His glory, where His love reveals itself and consumes all works in itself. In this manifestation you shall read your judgment and the terms of all that you have to do in this life; and then throw off all the heaviness which weighs you down, abandon all the meannesses that oppress you, and choose for yourself rather to live all your life far off from God than to accept any satisfaction that is less than God. All your perfection depends upon this: forsake every delight which is less than God, forsake every suffering which is not suffered only for His sake.

And yet indeed in all things you must have great compassion, though this for me is very hard. With a true will turn towards the highest truth. We have a true will when we refuse every consolation in heaven or on earth, in body or in soul, except only that for which God has loved us and has chosen us.

And let this be for you the highest good, and never turn to anyone for encouragement or consolation. Stand always ready to do its bidding, never failing, never paying heed to others: let them mock, let them approve, let them rail, let them bless, let them do as they like.

Never abandon the true life of good works, whether this seem bad or good to others. We can be glad to suffer the contempt which we earn with the good we do, when we know that they are God's will; and we can gladly suffer praise which we gain with those works of virtue in which God is glorified. The pains which our dear God suffered, when He lived as man on earth, merited that we should gladly suffer every pain and every contempt, and that we should long for pain of every kind. And the everlasting nature of His sweet love merits indeed that we should perform, with a perfect will, every work of virtue in which God, our love, is glorified.

Therefore you must not avoid contempt or blame. For everything which we can endure or perform is welcome to God's love, which can never be sated, for that love is the consuming fire which devours all things, and which never will be quenched in all eternity.

And because you are still young, and untried in all these things, you must strive greatly to grow up, as it were out of nothing, as one who has nothing and can become nothing but who yet labours to climb out of the depths. And you must always cast yourself deep into the abyss of humility, denying everything which you have to sacrifice to God. He asks this of you, that in all your dealings with all men you use a perfect humility. Raise yourself above everything which is inferior to God Himself, if you want

48

to be what He wants of you: and in doing this you will find peace in your whole being.

If you would act according to the being in which God has created you, your nature would be so noble that there would be no pains which you would shun, it would be so valiant that you could not bear to leave anything undone, but you would reach out for that which is best of all, for that great oneness which is God, knowing that to be your only riches. And then in mercy you must give your riches to others, and make rich those who are poor; for those who love truly will never fail in their free gifts to those others who with all their heart and all their will have surrendered themselves to God's love. True love has always given what it had to give, always conquered what it had to conquer, always withheld what it had to withhold.

Oh, now I ask you, my dear child, always to perform all the works of virtue which you have to do, never complaining, with a settled disposition towards them all, the little works and the great works. And do not ask and beg from God for anything, not for your own needs or for your friends, and do not ask Him for any sort of rest or consolation, but let Him give you what He pleases. Let Him come, let Him go, according to His holy will, and let Him do as is needful for His glory with you and with those to whom you would teach a loving submission to Him.

You may pray that His will be done both for yourself and for them; but you should not pray for them to have those things which they choose and decide for themselves. Nowadays most people go astray, deceiving themselves that sanctity is what they long for, when in reality they are taking their ease in second-rate consolations, more is the pity.

That is why you must choose and love God's will alone in all things. His will for you, for your friends, for Himself, even though your own wish might be for Him to give you consolation, so that you might live your life here in peace and rest.

But today, instead of loving God's will, everyone loves himself: it is everyone's will to have peace and rest, to live with God in riches and might, and to be one with Him in His joy and glory. We all want to be God along with God; but God knows that there are few of us who want to be man with Him in His humanity, to carry His Cross with Him, to hang upon it with Him, to pay with Him the debt of human kind. If we look at ourselves we can see that this is true: we will not suffer anything, we will not endure. Just let our hearts be stabbed by the slightest grief, just let someone say a scornful or slanderous word about us, let anyone act against our reputation or our peace or our will, and at once we are mortally injured: we know exactly what we want and what we do not want, there are so many different things which give us pleasure or pain, now we want this and now we want that, our joy today is our sorrow tomorrow, we would like to be here, we would like to be there, we do not want something and then we want it, and in everything all we are thinking of is our own satisfaction and how we can best seek it.

This is why we are still unenlightened in our thinking, unstable in all our being, uncertain in our reasoning and understanding. This is why we suffer so, poor wretched exiled beggars, painfully travelling through a foreign land, and there would be no need for this, were it not that all our thinking is false; and how false it is we show plainly when we do not live with Christ as He lived, do not abandon all as He did, are not abandoned by all as He was. If we look at what we do, we can see that this is true: whenever we can, we strive for our own ease, where we can gain it we fight for advancement, we fight to get our own way, we know exactly what is going to please us, we seek our own advantage in everything, in spiritual matters as well as worldly, and whatever we achieve in these ways, that is our joy and our delight, and when we have it we think that now we are something. And just as we say that, we are in truth nothing. This is how we destroy ourselves in our whole way of life, and we do not live with Christ and we do not carry the Cross with the Son of God. We only carry it with Simon, who was hired to carry the Cross of our Lord.

It is the same when we suffer and endure. We demand God as the reward for our good deeds, we want to know Him in this present life, because it seems to us that we are very deserving and that it is only right that He should give us some of what we ask in return for what we do. We think that what we do or suffer for Him is a great matter, and there is no rest for us until we have our reward and feel that we are pleasing to God, and what we would choose would be to have our reward here and now, a reward of consolation and rest in Him. And there is yet another reward which we choose, the reward of our own self-satisfaction and complacency. And our third reward is when we know that we are pleasing to others, and receive their respect and praise and honour.

All this is carrying the Cross with Simon, who laboured under the Cross for a short while, but did not die upon it. People who live in this way, even though to other men their lives may seem exalted and their works fine and splendid, so that sometimes they seem to live in wisdom and sanctity, well ordered and virtuous, have little about them which is pleasing to God, for they are neither upright nor enduring. The virtues which they seem to possess are in truth their failings; the most trifling opposition, if they encounter it, can expose them for what they are. One moment they are all exaltation and consolation, the next moment they are plunged into bitterness; because their lives are not built upon truth, their foundations are false and infirm. However much men may esteem them, in their works and in their lives they remain unstable and untrue. They are not upright, they are not persevering, and they do not die with Christ. They may perform the works of virtue, but their intention is neither pure nor true. There is so much falsehood mingled with their virtues that they can have no power to guide or illumine others, nor to persevere in a settled and firm truth, in which their everlastingness should be established.

For we are obliged to perform virtuous works not to gain admiration or happiness, not for wealth or power, nor for any pleasure in heaven or on earth, but only so that we may be pleasing to God's greatest honour, who created human nature for this, making it to His honour and His praise, and for our joy in eternal glory.

This is the way that the Son of God walked before us, the way which He showed and made known to us when He lived as a man. For all the time that He was on earth, from His beginning until the end, He performed and perfected in knowledge the will of His Father, in all He did, in all His days, with all that He was, with every service which He could do, in words, in works, in joy, in sorrow, in great things and little things, in miracles , in contempt, in suffering, in labour, in sorrow, in the anguish of His bitter death. With all His heart, with all His soul, with all His strength He stood ready to endure all things at all times to make perfect that which we had undone; and with all His might as God, and with all His goodness as man, He carried us and He drew us up, back to our first honourable state, back to that freedom in which we were created by a loving Creator, back to what we are now called to and chosen for in His predestination, to what He has foreseen from all eternity that we should be.

The mark of grace is holy living. The mark of predestination in an inward and confident lifting-up of the heart, with a living trustfulness, and with an unspeakable longing to honour and to satisfy Him in His glory, which is majestic and incomprehensible and divine.

The cross which we must carry with the living Son of God is that sweet exile which men suffer for their true love, when in a longing trustfulness we await that great day on which Love shall reveal itself and manifest its noble powers and its great might on earth and in heaven. Then Love shall show itself so mighty to those who love that it will draw them out of themselves, it will rob them of heart and mind, it will make them die and make them live in the loving service of true Love.

But before Love shall show itself so greatly, before it calls men so utterly to come out of themselves to it, before it so touches them that they become one spirit and one life with Love in Love, men must pay to Love the tribute of honourable service and a life of longing exile: honourable service in all the works of virtue, and a life of longing exile in perfect obedience, always standing ready with fresh zeal and willing hands for every deed in which virtue is exercised, with a will submissive to every virtue which can pay honour to Love. And in all this there must be no other intention than that Love should be enthroned, as it should be, in men and in all creatures, according to Love's pleasure. This is to hang upon the Cross with Christ, this is to die with Him and with Him to rise again. May He help us always to do this; and for this help I entreat Him in whom is every perfect virtue.

LETTER 7

My dear one, I greet you with that love which God is, with what I am, which is in part what God is. And I thank you for what you are, and I reprove you for what you are not. Oh, my dear, we must use ourselves to fight our opponents, finding strength to pit against their strength, cunning against cunning, power against power, love against love, all that we are against all that they are, always opposing like to like; if we contend so, we may be content, and otherwise not. It is Love alone which contends against us, Love alone which can content us. Every hour of the day, we must contend against Love and find fresh force to use against it, with all our strength, all our cunning, all our power, all our love, with all we are; and all we are is our delight in Love.

You whom I love, never forget to serve Love in fresh works, and leave Love to work, even though we feel that what we do cannot delight Love nor content it. Love is sufficient to itself, even though we are insufficient to attain it. Love always brings its own rewards, though sometimes it brings them late. Whoever gives all that he is to Love shall have all that Love is, whether that be for him sorrow or joy.

LETTER 8

As Love grows between the two who love, so there grows in love a dread, and this dread is of two natures. The first dread is when men fear that they are not worthy of such a love, and that they cannot do enough for it. This dread is a most noble dread. In this dread men grow greatly, and in it they become wholly subject to Love. With this dread in them, men stand ready to fulfill the commandments of Love. Such a dread preserves them in humility, for it fosters in them a watchfulness and a courageousness. For when they fear that they may not be worthy of so great a love, their whole nature is shaken and they are robbed of all their rest. They long to suffer for Love, and so they learn all the fine usages of Love, for they fear lest their words should be too churlish to reach the ears of Love. In this dread they are set free, for they can think of nothing else, feel nothing else than their longing to be pleasing to Love. So in this dread those who love are adorned. Dread makes their minds clear, counsels their heart, purifies their conscience, gives wisdom to their spirit, unites their faculties, watches over their works and their words, makes them so bold that they shrink from no death. These are the gifts of that dread which dreads not to be sufficient for Love.

The second dread is when men fear that Love does not love them enough. Because Love has bound them captive so fast, it seems to them that Love is constantly laying fresh burdens upon them, is never helping them enough, that they love and are not loved in return. Such mistrust is better than the most perfect trust; and by trust I mean a love which satisfies but which is blind, a trust which can be satisfied with what it possesses here and now. But this noble mistrust breaks the conscience wide open. Even if a man loves till he fears that he is going mad, till his heart grows sick, till the blood chills in his veins and his soul perishes, if it is true Love which he so loves, this noble mistrust prevents him from feeling or trusting Love, for his longing for Love and his lack of trust have broken his heart wide open. Mistrust renews longing, for he can never be sure, but always he fears that he is not loved enough by Love. This is the power of that mistrust, when a man always fears that he does not love enough and that he is not loved enough.

The man who feels such imperfections in himself and wishes to emend them must strive with his whole heart to achieve in all things a perfect trust. All sufferings must be pleasing to him for Love: he must not seek to justify himself with ready answers, but what he does for Love he must keep to himself, and he must be silent when he longs to speak, and when he longs for the silent contemplation of his delight he must speak, so that men do not reproach Love with his love. And he should rather suffer beyond his powers of endurance, than that he should fail in the smallest observance which is to the honour of Love.

Men must put out of their hearts all anger, to make place for the peace of true Love, even if this meant loving the devil himself. Whoever loves is obliges to forsake all things and to despise himself as the most wretched of all men, so as to pay due honour to the excellence of Love. Whoever loves, let him gladly submit to the judgment of men without selfexculpation, if he wants to be the more free in his love; and he will be glad to suffer many things for the sake of love. Whoever loves will gladly be chastised, so that he may be taught. Whoever loves will readily be disowned, so that he may be utterly free. Whoever loves will joyfully be alone, so that he may love and possess his Love.

There is little more than I can say to you now, because of my many cares, some of which you know, some of which you cannot know. If it might be, I would gladly say more to you. My heart is oppressed and sick, and that is partly because I have not yet a perfect trust. When Love stirs my soul, I shall say more to you of these things than I have said till now.

LETTER 9

May God make you know, dear child, what He is and how He uses His servants, and especially His handmaidens; and may He consume you in Himself. There where the profundity of His wisdom is, there shall He teach you what He is, and how wonderfully sweet it is for the beloved to dwell in his Love, and how Love so dwells in all the beloved that neither can perceive difference between them. But they possess one another in a mutual possession, their mouths one mouth, their hearts one heart, their bodies one body, their souls one soul, and sometimes one sweet divine nature transfuses them both, and they are one, each wholly in the other, and yet each one still remains and always will remain himself.

LETTER 10

Whoever loves God loves His works. His works are the noble virtues. Therefore, whoever loves God loves virtue. This is a love which is true and full of consolation. It is virtue which is the proof of love, not the sweetness of devotion. For sometimes it happens that there are men who love little but feel much sweetness. It is not by what they feel that men's love is to be measured, but by their being founded upon virtue and rooted in charity.

In our longing for God we sometimes taste sweetness; but not all of this comes from Him, for it proceeds more from our own sensibilities than from grace, more from nature than from the spirit. To feel such sweetness is to feel the soul   stirred, but this is more a lesser good, it is less a greater good, and it gives more pleasure than it gives profit, for it reflects rather the nature of men than the nature of Love.

The imperfect experience this kind of sweetness as well as the perfect. The imperfect think that they have found great love, because they taste great sweetness, but it is not pure but alloyed. And even if this sweetness is pure and wholly from God, it is difficult to be sure of this, and our love is not to be measured in this way, but as we possess virtue and charity, as you have heard.

For we can observe in such souls that so long as sweetness lasts in them, they are in fine fettle, but once sweetness is gone their love is gone, and then they are in a fearful state. This is because they are not yet possessed by virtues. Because if virtues are early implanted in the soul and are firmly rooted there by long exercise, when sweetness vanishes the virtues act according to their nature and continue to perform the works of Love. They do not wait for sweetness, but they are concerned how faithfully they can do service for Love. They do not hanker after pleasure, but they watch for profit. They work for the sake of the work and not for wages. They confide everything to Love, and ask for nothing better. Love is so noble and so gentle that no one can give them more. Let no one grumble at what he is paid: if he has done his share, Love will indeed do its share. The wise, who always stand in the service of virtues, know this well. They seek, each one, to do the will of Love; and they ask Love for no other sweetness than to show them in all things what is the dearest will of Love. If they are lifted up in joy, let that be according to Love's will; if they are plunged into sorrow, Love's will be done.

But there are other souls who are poor in virtues. When they feel sweetness, they feel love, but when sweetness departs their love departs with it. In the day of grace they are bold, but in the night of tribulation they turn and run. Such people have little courage; they are easily exalted in bliss, easily cast down into bitterness. The smallest consolation fills their hearts with joy, the merest grief oppresses them greatly.

This is why it sometimes happens that men of unstable heart are more easily moved than the constant, those who are poor in grace more easily than the rich. Because when God comes with His graces, and wants to console them in their pusillanimity, and to help their weakness and to bolster up their will, they are filled with joy in Him and longing for His sweetness, and they are far more moved than are those who are constantly filled with His grace. And at times like this people think that such men have great grace and great love, when in truth they are poor indeed. So it is that sometimes it is the lack of God, rather than the fullness of Him, which is the cause of sweetness.

Then there are times when it is the evil spirit who is the cause of sweetness. For sometimes a man will experience sweetness and feel such delight in it that he is wholly occupied with his delight, and falls into bodily sickness, and neglects the means which could help him. And sometimes when a man feels that he is filled to overflowing with such great sweetness, little by little he comes to believe that he is already perfect, and so he leaves off trying to make his life more perfect.

So that it is very necessary that each man should carefully preserve the grace which is given to him, that he should prudently nurture the gifts of our Lord. For the gifts of grace do not justify a man, they obligate him: if he uses his graces he will be pleasing to God, and if he does not he is a debtor. And he must also use discretion in the exercise of his graces. Virtue can lose its virtue if it be not used at the proper time; and just so grace is no longer grace if it is not exercised according to the precepts of grace.

Therefore the man whom God has made the steward of His goods must be prudent and so administer His grace that it is not lost to him. For just as the man who is lacking grace must ask God for grace, so the man who has grace must ask Him to preserve it. For as often as a man allows those riches of our Lord which are in him to dwindle and not to increase, he has forfeited them, were it not for the goodness of God.

This is why the Bride of whom we read in the Song of Songs says that she has sought her Beloved not only with longing but also with prudence; and when she had found Him she did not cease anxiously to keep Him with her.

So would every prudent soul do which was moved by Love. Such a soul would constantly increase its grace, longingly and prudently, anxiously tilling its land, uprooting the weeds and planting virtues and building there the dwelling of a clean conscience, into which it could worthily receive its beloved.

LETTER II

Ah, dear child, may God give you what my heart longs that you should have: and that would be for you to love God as He deserves. And yet, dear child, I have never been able to endure the thought that anyone before me could have loved Him so dearly as I. Yet of course I believe that there were many who have loved Him as much and as dearly, even though I could not suffer to think that anyone could have known Him or loved Him so greatly as I.

Since I was ten years old, I have been so possessed by a whole-hearted love for God that in the first two years when I began to love Him so, I should have died, had He not given me greater strength than most people have, and given to my nature the power of His nature; and often He gave me counsel, which sometimes was illumined with many gracious shewings; and I received from Him many wonderful gifts in which I felt and I saw what He is. And in all these tokens of love which I felt between Him and me, according to the usages of love, just as lovers use between themselves, concealing little, giving much, finding most in their close communion one with another, each one as it were tasting all, eating all, drinking all, consuming all the other, in all these tokens which God my Love so plentifully gave to me at the beginning of my life, He gave me trust in Him, that from then on I generally felt that no one had loved Him with so whole a heart as I. But there were times when reason said indeed to me that I was not the one who loved Him best. But though I thought this, I could never feel it or believe it, so closely was I bound to Him in the bonds of true Love.

So this is how I am now: in the end, I cannot believe that I have loved Him best, and yet I cannot believe that there is any living man who loves God as I love Him. So sometimes Love illumines me so that I know how far short I fall, that I am not enough for my Love, that I do not love Him as He deserves; and at times the sweet nature of Love grants me so to taste and to feel Love that I am blinded, that that suffices me, that I am so rich in being together with Love that I confess to Love that Love alone suffices me.

LETTER 12

May God be God to you, and may you love Him. God grant to you that you may live only to do all those works of love which are fitting to Love. So I begin in that true humility in which she who loved Him best began, with which she drew Him down into her. So must everyone do who wishes to draw God down into him and rejoice in Him in Love. There must be no earthly thing which can exalt him, there must be no earthly task which can occupy him: he must always be strong when he is afflicted, always insistent in seeking, always constant in finding. You ask me to write of these things, but you know them all well yourself, what one must do to be perfect before God.

Those who wait and long to love God to His satisfaction begin here on earth the life of eternity, in which they will live with God for ever. To requite His love and to suffice it is the unceasing labour of all heaven and all earth, and it will never be ended. For that Love so exalted and so great which is God will never be exhausted and never be comprehended, however much we may strive to that end; and all the blessed in heaven must eternally burn in the never-failing fire of their loving longing to requite that Love. And so those who on earth are satisfi ed with nothing else, and who accept no other consolation than their constant striving to requite Love, they begin here that life of eternity in which the blessed are with God in their delight in Love.

Every idea which comes to man's mind about God, everything which he can understand, all the images which he can form, none of this is God Himself. For if man could comprehend and understand Him with his senses and intellect, God would be less than man and man's love for Him would soon be perfected; you can see this among earthly men, who love so quickly and are so soon out of love.

In a few words, these are all they who are not bound in the bonds of eternal Love, who do not always keep watch in their hearts in order to requite Love. But those who wait upon Love to requite it, they themselves are eternal and boundless; for all their conversation is in heaven, and their souls are drawn after that Love which is itself boundless. Yet even though they love the Beloved with an eternal love, still they will never be possessed by the whole of Love, because they themselves cannot possess the whole of Him whom they love, can never requite Him, even though that is all that they long for; they long to requite Him or else to perish as they strive, and for nothing else do they strive.

So I command you, and I exhort you in the name of that true Love which is God that you hasten towards Love, and that you help us all to love Him, this I beg you above all other things. Think without ceasing upon the goodness of God, mourn that you have attained to so little of it, mourn that He in His blessedness rejoices in it, whilst we in our exile are so far off from it, when He and those who love Him are filled so full of it, rejoice so greatly in it, and in His goodness flow in and flow out again in all goodness. Oh that great God, whom we cannot comprehend through any labour of our own, may that true Love which is He help us to come to Him! It is His Love which brings Him down to us, that lets us feel a little what He is, and this is how men can know Him. This is riches rich beyond all telling, and yet, God knows, still in such riches there remains for us some woe. Yet for those who are governed by the court of Love, Love's rule must be that they find their deepest rest in labouring for their Love, in paying Him the honours which content Him, in gaining the rewards of faithful lovers, no earthly reward but only that Love may always be requited and be reward enough for us.

But nowadays Love is too often hindered, its laws are too often broken through lawlessness. No one will ever forgo his earthly satisfactions, for the honour of Love. They want to hate and to love to their heart's content, to quarrel and make up as they please, and not according to the laws of brotherly love. They are ashamed to keep Love's laws, and so they show how weak they are. They break its laws in their intemperateness, and this is a wrong which brings many injuries. The first is that wisdom is so forgotten. The second is that brotherhood is so impaired. The third is that the Holy Spirit is so driven out. The fourth is that the devil is so encouraged. The fifth is that friendship is so disrupted, and remains concealed and forgotten. The sixth is that virtue is so neglected. The seventh is that justice is so impaired.

The sin of hatred and of a zeal which is alien from the Spirit of God and no holy zeal, this vice robs us of Love and of our noble desires, it destroys purity, it makes us watch our brethren with suspicion, it deprives us of the sweetness of the love that we should feel for them; and those who are moved by envy forget to live the life of heaven, but always they live the life of hell.

The sin of seeking wordly consolations makes men forget the narrow way which leads to an exalted Love, and all its lovely life and its sweet conduct and the well-ordered usages which are fitting for a Love exalted above all.

Through the sin of frivolous affection men forget that humility which is the most honourable state and the purest chamber in which they can receive Love. And in this sin they lose that illumined reason which is our rule, which teaches us what we should do under the law of Love, when men wish to requite that Love. For illumined reason lightens all the ways in which we must serve exalted Love according to its dearest will, and it shows clearly all the life which is satisfying to that Love. Alas, that these two, reason and humility, should be driven out by frivolous affection is the most lamentable pity that I know and which can ever happen.

These sins which I have shown to you all injure and hinder the true law of Love. And from these capital sins of which I have spoken, countless lesser sins derive, and they all rob us of the light of Love. Even if you and others are not afflicted by these greatest sins, there are many others which creep into you, disguising themselves as fine virtues so that you will not take fright and drive them out. Arrogance will come disguised as humility, oppression as rightfulness, envy as loyalty and reason, vain joy as consolation and trust, false love as good sense and patience, as confidence and good counsel, which yet never came to you from God. From all this no man can shield himself who is not shielded in the bonds of true Love.

Understand well that I have not said this in reproach of you, but to warn you of the harms which can come to us from these and other sins which we cannot escape. And it seems lamentable to us that one person should bring harm to another, as those injure us who do not help us in loving our Beloved. But because you have office in the community which will enable you sometimes to help or to hinder others in this matter, I have warned you to keep watch on yourself and on others, so that Love's just laws are kept at all times. And with all the power that is in you, show to others the signs of Love, in all things and above all things.

For the hardest word that I know in the Scriptures is the commandment of Love which God gave to Moses: 'You must love the Lord your God with all your heart, with all your soul, with all your strength.' And when He had said this, He then went on:

'You must never forget these words, sleeping or waking. If you sleep, you must dream of this; when you are awake, you must think it, speak it, do it. You must write these words upon the doorpost and upon the lintel and on the wall and in every place where people can come, so that they can never forget what they have to do, which is, never to forget Love, sleeping or waking, in any way, as God Himself has commanded, with all that they are, with heart, with soul, with mind, with strength, with thought. So God commanded, to Moses and in the Gospel, that we must be wholly given over to Love. Ah, how dare we then ever be anything less to Love? Is it not a dreadful reproach to us that we keep anything from Love, hold anything back? Think of this, strive for this, never forget it, do the work of Love in all things.

Remember also what the prophet Abdias says: the house of Jacob must be a fire, the house of Joseph must be a flame, and Esau's house shall be stubble. Jacob is the man who conquers: through the power of love he conquers God, so that God may conquer him. And after he has conquered, so that he may be conquered and receive a blessing, he must help others to be conquered who are not yet fully conquered, and who still walk straight on both feet, not limping as do those who have become Jacob. For Jacob was injured in the fight, and was always afterwards lame on one side, and it was only after he had been lamed and conquered that he was given the blessing. So must all men be who wish to become Jacob and to receive God's blessing. Whoever wishes to contend with God, let him strive to conquer so that he may be conquered. And he must limp on one side, where there might be something else for him than God alone, or where there is something which means more to him than God. Whoever has something which means more to him than God, whoever is not one with Him in His single and sweet blessing, he walks on two feet and is unconquered, and he receives no blessing. You must so entirely abandon yourself for God's sake that you burn ardently in your unity with Him, in all your life and in all your works, so that you have nothing else than God alone, so that you know neither joy nor sorrow, neither ease nor toil. And when you live this life without ceasing, then Jacob's house has become a fire.

Joseph's house must be a flame. Just as Joseph was a protector and a guide to his people and to his brothers, so must you and those who have become Joseph be leaders and guardians to the others who are not yet grown to this, who still fall short of what they ought to be. With the fire of your own burning life you must ignite them, with the flame of your burning love you must illumine them.

Most people are strangers, are Esau, and their house is stubble, which will be consumed with the fiery flames. So others must be fired by you, when you are so enflamed. This is part of your office as a superior: you must set fire to the dry stubble with good example and conduct, with prayers and counsel and warnings. You must guide your brethren with inward love, and help them to love, so that they love in God and in righteous works for Him and in proper virtues. And always remember what the Scriptures say: '*Sobrie, pie, iuste vivamus in hoc seculo*', 'Let us live soberly, lovingly, justly in this world.' This is part of your office.

Oh, help us with your pure love for God alone, so that our Beloved may be loved. All in all, this is what I want above all things for you: a proper love towards God. I admonish you, I beg you to give that to God, and then let Him make perfect what is lacking in us.

God be with you; hasten towards Love.

LETTER 13

Man must preserve himself in innocency among all earthly things, so that he may seek to grow in all things, and work according to the just precepts of reason above all things. And so in everything which he does God will go before him and go with him, and he with God will perform all just works; and he will long for God to perfect all the righteous works of His nature in him and in us all. To choose this and to want this above all things, this is the law which governs a loving heart, whether what it chooses bring it curse or blessing. The loving heart will always long and always pray to be at unity with Love, as we read in the Song of Songs: '*Dilectus meus mihi et ego illi*', 'My Beloved is mine and I am His.' So we shall all be united into one will of our only Love.

Whoever wishes for all things to be subjected to him must subject himself to his reason, above anything which he can wish for or which anyone can wish for him. For no one can become perfect in Love except him who is subjected to reason. For reason loves God for His great nature, and noble natures love Him to be loved by Him, and baser natures love Him for their needs. Therefore each man must do everything which is possible to him in all things, as is required of him by the perfection of Love, which can never be statisfied, however much we give. Even though a man's life may be such that in other men's eyes he may seem pleasing to God, still he comes so far short of what the perfect satisfaction of Love requires, that he must always be spurred on by Love and long greatly to do more than he yet can.

Love is best satisfied when man is utterly deprived of any rest which he could find, in strangers, in friends, in Love itself. This is a fearful life which Love demands, that we must forgo the satisfactions of Love in order to satisfy Love. Those whom Love has so seized and drawn and grasped, they will never be free of the debt which Love in the great power of its violent nature imposes on them, always to be ready to satisfy Love. That life is a misery more than the human heart can bear.

For nothing in such men's lives contents them, no gift, no service, no comfort, nothing which they can do. For Love within them draws them so powerfully towards it, and they feel Love to be so immense and so incomprehensible, and then they find themselves to be so petty and so impotent to satisfy that life which is Love. And they know that they are altogether bound to satisfy Love with their whole life, so that they can find neither sorrow nor joy in any other thing, in any other man or in themselves, but only in that which Love alone is. In Love they can find their joy and sorrow: joy, when Love is fostered and grows in them and in others; sorrow, when Love is harmed or wounded in those who love, in themselves and in those others whom strangers are so glad to harm and to wound when they can.

Labour that Love may be fostered, labour for great charity's sake; for charity understands all God's commandments without error, and keeps them without labour. Whoever loves need not labour, for what he does feels not like labour to him. The more burningly we love, the better we hasten and the faster we come to God's sanctity, which is Himself, and to His totality, which is Himself. In His totality may all your service be perfected, and your devotion, which His perfection demands and which is satisfying to His whole nature, which is wholly loving. May He give you to see the whole debt which you owe to Him, the sufferings which you must offer to Him, and above all the single love which He commands that we should love Him with.

LETTER 14

May God be for you His great and eternal Love, may He grant you the grace to live wisely and to achieve that incomparable virtue which is of satisfaction to His holy Love. Labour for this every hour of your life without ceasing, Always be utterly humble, and serve wisely. God help you and comfort you in your whole life, and teach you those true virtues with which we best pay honour to Love and best live justly. May God teach you that well-pleasing unity with His Father which He offered to Him when He lived here on earth as man, though in His purity unlike any other man. And may He instruct you in that holy unity which He taught and commanded to His holy friends, who forsook all other consolations for the love of God. And may He make you know, in your true belief and in your works, that dear sweet unity which still He teaches His dear friends to know, when they urge themselves on, above all other things, to His sweet and holy Love.

See to it that you are always renewed, fresh and never wearying; and recollect that exalted life of eternal love of which St Paul speaks, telling us what are its marks, what it is and what it can perform; and found yourselves in that. This is what you must always do, if you are to live for God, for anything which we do without love is as nothing. Therefore hasten to pursue that love, with the power of ardent longing for your true Love. Be bold in love, be constant in this life's pilgrimage, and end your wanderings and arrive in the joys of the land of Love, in which love shall last for ever. Love is the humility which we owe, for whoever knows that he does not yet possess the riches of the love of God must humble himself under the mighty power of God.

It is indeed just that He who is all to those whom He loves should require them to be all to Him, as the Bride says in the Song of Songs: 'My love is mine, and I am His.' To whom should one be anything except to the loved one? Everything which one gives to others, except only the love one gives to the beloved, is an exchange between strangers. But the exchange of love alone is sweet and blessed in all things.

If you want to know this perfection, first of all you must learn to know yourself, your dealings, your wishes, your aversions, your actions, your love, your hate, your trust, your mistrust, everything which you do. You must test yourself, how well you can endure what is displeasing to you, how well you can renounce what you love. This is the greatest trial which a young heart can endure, to renounce what it would gladly accept. Test yourselves in everything which is agreeable to you, what use you make of it, how reasonably and how moderately you regard it. In everything which happens to you, preserve equanimity: in calm and in suffering. Prudently see what were the deeds of our Lord; from them you must learn perfection. It is very fitting that each man should scrutinize, wisely and prudently, God's graces and riches. For God has given man the fine gift of reason, to teach him in all his ways and illumine him in all his works, and if man would follow the counsels of reason, he would never be deceived.

LETTER 15

Nine things are needful for a pilgrim who has far to travel. First, he must ask the way. Second, he must choose good companions. Third, he must guard against thieves. Fourth, he must guard against excess. Fifth, he must hitch up his clothes and belt them in fast. Sixth, as he climbs mountains, he must stoop. Seventh, as he comes downhill, he must walk upright. Eighth, he must ask for good men's prayers. Ninth, he must be glad to talk about God.

So it is with our spiritual pilgrimage, in which we must seek God's kingdom and His righteousness in the perfect works of Love.

The first point is that you must ask the way. God Himself says: 'I am the way.' Ah, since He is the way, look at the way on which He travelled: how He laboured and burned within in love, how outwardly He performed the works of virtue to strangers and to friends; and listen how He commanded men how much they ought to love their God with all their heart, with all their soul, with all their strength, and that they should never forget this, sleeping or waking. See how He did just as He taught, who yet Himself was God, how He gave all and how He lived wholly for the true Love of His Father and for His love for men. He laboured with a love that never slept, and He gave to Love all His heart and all His soul and all His strength. This is the way

69

which Jesus points, and which He is Himself, and which He Himself walked, the way where lies eternal life and joy in the truth of His Father's glory.

Then ask the way from His saints, from those whom He has called to Him, and those who still remain here and who follow Him in perfect virtue, who have followed Him up into the mountain of exaltation out of the deep valley of humility, who have climbed that high mountain with firm faith and great confidence as they contemplate that fervent and sweet Love.

And ask the way from those who are with you and whom you see to be following Him most closely, and who are obedient to Him in all the works of virtue. So follow Him who is Himself the way, and them who have followed and still follow Him.

The second point is that you must choose good company. That is the holy community in which you share in so much goodness, and, above all, it is the holy lovers of God by whom He is most loved and honoured, and by whom you feel that you can best be helped, with whom your heart is most united and exalted to God, and whose words and company draw you and help you most to God. But by no means seek in this your own repose and gratification. And look closely at me and at all the others in whom you seek to repose your trust, see what we are, see if you are improved by us, see what our life is. For there are very few upon earth in whom you can fully trust; for almost everyone nowadays wants, from God and from men, only what will please them, only what they yearn for, and if they do not get it they suffer.

The third point is that you must be on your guard against thieves. These are the subtle temptations which come to you from without and within. No one can learn a trade without a master, and you must not be so rash as to undertake any extra-ordinary way of life without the advice of those prudent in spiritual matters.

The fourth point is that you must be on your guard against excess. Guard against finding repose in things alien from God, let nothing but Him content you, taste nothing else until you taste how wonderfully sweet God is. Always think and always be sure that if anything but God alone suffices us, that is excess.

The fifth point is that you must hitch up your clothes and belt them in tight. That is to shield yourself from every earthly stain and every baseness, and to be girded so well with the bond of that Love which is God that you let yourself sink down to nothing lower than He.

The sixth point is that as you climb the mountain you must stoop down low. That is to give thanks for all the sufferings which come to you for the sake of Love, and that you humble yourself with your whole heart, even if you could perform as many works of virtue as all the men alive; still you must seem to yourself little and nothing in comparison with God's greatness and with all the debt you owe to Him of service and of love.

The seventh point is that as you go downhill you must walk upright. That is that even though from time to time you must sink to accept what you feel that your bodily nature needs and requires, still you must hold up your longing towards God, along with those holy ones who lived in the heights and who said: 'All our conversation is in heaven.'

The eighth point is that you must ask for the prayers of good men. That is that you must ask all the saints and all men to help you to come to the perfect will of God, and you must forsake all things, to be one with them in God.

The ninth point is that you must be glad to talk about God. It is a sign of love that the Beloved's name is sweet. St Bernard says of this: 'Jesus is honey in the mouth.' It is sweet beyond sweetness to speak of the Beloved, and it stirs the soul to its depths, and it makes easy the works of Love.

Now I admonish you by God's holy Love, that you go on your pilgrimage: let it be pleasing, let it be seemly, let no selfwill injure or afflict you, go on it in a sweet and peaceful joy of the spirit. Travel through this land of exile so straight and so pure and so ardent that in the end you find God, your Beloved, and to this end may He help you and His holy Love.

God be with you; and may He teach you the true ways which are proper to His exalted Love. Be prompt and wise in what you have to do, earnest as you search your heart and as you search for Him, and firm in your faith; and so may you seek truly not for your own gratification but for God's will, and so shall you obtain all that He in His love intends for you.

And you must also live in great hope, which will come from your firm trust in God, that He will grant you to love Him with the great Love with which He loves Himself, in Trinity and unity, that Love in which He has from all eternity been sufficient to Himself and eternally will be so.

All heavenly beings are busy to requite Him with this Love, and always will be so. That is their office, which will never be completed. There is no sweeter delight than to know that we fall short of that delight. And earthly beings must stand ready, with humble hearts, and they must know that before so great a Love, so exalted a Love, so unrequited a Beloved, they and their loves are too puny to be of satisfaction. Oh, this labour that can never be perfected, that must shake every loving soul to its depths, must make it reject everything unnecessary to this labour, everything inimical to it, everything smaller than a love to requite God's love.

Where two things are to be joined into one, there must be nothing between them except the substance which is to unite them. This substance is Love, uniting God and the blessed soul. Holy Love every hour is exhorting those noble ones to have this great trust, to understand this, to throw aside everything for the sake of Love, as He threw everything aside when He was sent by His Father and when He made perfect the work which Love had commanded Him to do, as He said Himself in the Gospel: 'Father, the hour has come.' With this He said to His Father: 'I have perfected the work which You gave me to do.'

Now see how He lived, and the saints who came after Him, and the good men alive today, and all those who wish to do the works of that great Love which is God. Always they live with humble hearts, zealous without flagging in the performance of good works. Live according to righteousness, not for your own satisfaction or pleasure, but only so far as you know that what you do is to His glory, is according to His law, is well pleasing to Him. Trust in His great goodness as a child trusts its father. Be prompt to follow counsel which is good and which is given to you by your friends who are anxious for your betterment. And listen gladly to anyone else who gives you counsel which will help you towards virtue; and suffer gladly everything which you must bear for the sake of Love.

You are too fainthearted and too childish in everything you do. In all your actions, you are too quickly depressed and put out of mood. What is the use of being at the mercy of every trifle? Reserve yourself for only the honour of God, strive to labour for it; idleness is a grave fault in those who want to imitate God, because idleness is the mistress of all mischief. Pray constantly, or perform works of love and virtue, or serve the sick; for the honour of Love, suffer with the irascible and the ignorant. Be joyful in the Spirit of God, because God alone is sufficient to Himself and He is Love. Always be pleasant in your community, and let all their sufferings be your own, as St Paul says: 'Who is sick, and I am not?' Weigh your every word as if it were spoken before Christ Himself. who is the truth.

It may grieve you that I preach so much to you about duties of which you are well aware and which you carry out. But I do this as an admonition of the truth, that whoever wishes to gain Love must begin with virtue, as God Himself did and sall His saints; for we read of the martyrs that with faith they conquered kingdoms. It is not said that they did this with Love. That is because faith establishes Love; but Love enkindles faith. So the works of faith must precede Love, and Love will enkindle them. So be content with this, for I have written it to you in good will.

> Seek after every virtue with a gracious zeal
> Yet look to no one virtue for your all-in-all.
> In nothing be found wanting,
> Want nothing more than everything.
> Towards every man's need show grace and pity,
> Yet take no one under your special protection.
> For long I have wanted to say this to you,
> For it lay very heavily upon my heart.
> May God show you what it is I mean
> In the solitary nature of Love alone.

These things, which I forbid to you in these words, were forbidden to me by God. And that is why I am bound to forbid them to you, so that you may perfectly be a part of Love's perfection, so that you may be perfectly and wholly one with the Divine Being. For the attributes of that Being which I have named here are perfectly that Being's nature. For grace and zeal are of the nature of the Holy Spirit; they are the properties of His Person. And not to look upon one thing with more favour than upon another, that is the nature of the Father, and in this He is the only Father. This giving-out, this holding-back, this is the pure Divinity, this is the whole nature of Love.

> In nothing be found wanting,
> Want nothing more than everything.

What I say here first signifies the might of the Father, for He is God omnipotent. And what I say next betokens His just will, in

74

which His justice works its secret, mighty works, those works which remain deep and dark, hidden and concealed from all those who are, as I said, inferior to God's unity, who still are in service, however well they may serve, to the separate qualities of the different Persons, as I say in the first lines of these couplets: seeking after every virtue with gracious zeal, being found wanting in nothing, showing grace and pity to every man's need. And yet this seems to be the most perfect life that one can live upon earth, and you have always heard me recommending this life above all others, and I sought myself to live it rather than any other, and I served it reverently and I worked in this way, until the day when it was forbidden to me.

But in the second lines of these couplets I tell of the perfection in which the unity of the Persons and Love are one, and how They, according to the justness of Their own being, act as if They were one Person and one Love and nothing else. Oh God, how terrible a life is this, in which such contraries, such hating and such loving, are together devoured!

'Towards every man's need show grace and pity': that referred to the Son, and to the qualities of His person; so He was and so He did and all was well done. 'Yet take no one under your special protection': Such special protection, that great and heavy labour which God performed for His Son, is always for the Father alone to do. And this is the loveliest attribute of Love in the Divinity; this attribute is so full of Love's justice that it absorbs into itself all the zeal, all the humanity, all the force with which we long not to fall short of any man's needs of us. It absorbs the love and the compassion which we feel for those in Hell and in Purgatory, for those who know nothing of God, for whose who know Him but who yet suffer because they do not perform His dearest will, and for those who love Him and who yet endure more than all these others, because they lack Him whom they love. Love's justice absorbs all this into itself; and yet each Person has given out His own attribute, as I have said.

But that just and single nature in which Love is itself in Love and in perfect delight, that nature is not occupied in virtue nor in the exercises of virtues nor in any particular activities, however excellent they be, however great their authority; nor is that nature troubled by the needs of any man, great though its power is to help him.

For in the delight of Love there never was, there never can be any other act than that delight alone, in which delight it is that the unique omnipotent Divinity is Love.

What God forbade to me, as I have said, was upon earth to love anything else than Him; I was to have no regard for anything but Love, and so to give myself to the service of Love that everything which is foreign to Love might be hated and avoided by me, that I in my delight in Love should no longer feel any inclination towards good, no longer do any particular work for Love, no longer feel compassion for Love or long to protect it, but always, unceasingly, to live in the delight of Love. But when we feel that delight sink and dwindle in us, then are we bound and allowed to do these three things which at other times are forbidden.

Whilst we seek for Love and serve Love, we may do all things to the honour of love, for during this time we are human and necessitous. Then we may well perform every kind of work, and give, and serve, and feel pity, for at such times we lack everything, we need everything. But when in the delight of Love we are united with God we then become God, sharing His power and His justice; and then will and work and power are alike just, and these are the three Persons in one God.

All this was forbidden to me on the feast of the Ascension, four years ago, by God the Father Himself, at the moment when His Son became flesh upon the altar. And at His coming He kissed me, and in this sign it was shown to me that I was one with Him, and so I came with Him before His Father; and the Father received Him in me and me in Him. And in this unity into which

I had been brought and in which I had been illumined, I understood God's being and comprehended it more clearly than men may say, or think, or see any earthly thing which is so comprehensible.

This seems indeed a wonderful thing. But even though I say that it seems wonderful, I know very well that there is nothing for you to wonder at. For the kingdom of this earth cannot understand heavenly things; for people can reason about everything upon earth and find language enough for it, but I can find neither language nor reason for this. I may be able to reason as well as any other, but still I can find no language for what I have said to you, for I know that there are no words for it.

Even though there are some things I command you not to do, some things I commend to your doing, you can still be of service in many things. But in all that I have said to you, I forbid to you just what was forbidden to me in God's will. But you can still labour in the works of Love, as I did for long, as His friends did and still do, and as I did a little for a while and still always do; place your reliance upon nothing but Love, do no other works than the works of Love, take nothing but Love under your protection, serve in no other service than the service of Love. What else you must do, what else you must eschew, may God, our Love, show you.

LETTER 18

Oh, my sweet child, my dear child, be wise in God. For you have great need of wisdom, as has every man who wants to become like to God. For wisdom leads us very deep into God. But nowadays no one wants to learn, no one can learn what are his duties in that service to Love which he owes. Indeed, you have much to do, if you are in this life to know Christ as God and as man, if you are to grow to that full stature which is fitting to the excellence for which God has in His love chosen you. In everything which

77

happens to you be wise and bold and unafraid, in everything which you do act as befits your noble calling.

God, who is powerful beyond all power and mighty, gives plentifully to all men, according to His power and His grace, not according to their efforts or their achievements or to their own gifts, but according to His rich omnipotence and according to His mighty commands, which are the manifestations of His perfection. These serve Him, they rule His kingdom, they give to every man what he has need of, as is required to the glory and the satisfaction of Him who is Lord over all. Each of them gives according to its nature and its office. Mercy gives to those poor who live in perfect poverty, whenever it finds them ensnared in vices and afflicted because of their humility and poverty. Charity watches over the commoners of God's kingdom, and gives to each one what he needs. Wisdom arrays all His fine knights for the great battles and fierce attacks in which they must fight in their burning longing for their one true Love. Perfection gives to His magnates rule over their estates, like the great power of those mighty souls of whom I spoke, who with a will powerful and perfected and with perfect works have gained every freedom and every favour which Love's will can grant.

But it is Justice which endows with these four virtues, it is Justice which shall condemn or approve. This is how the emperor himself preserves his freedom and his peace, by enjoining his officers to keep justice, and he endows his kings and his dukes and his counts and his princes with the rich rewards of his greatness, with the fine prizes decreed in the laws of Love, who is the crown of every noble soul which knows how to be of help to every man in his needs without ever diminishing its own love for its Beloved. This is what I meant when I recently wrote to you, concerning the three virtues, 'Towards every man's need show grace and pity, yet take no one under your special protection', and what else I then said to you.

So you must do your best to preserve this noble perfection

78

of your fine, perfected soul. And consider what this means. You must remain undivided, you must not be concerned with good or with evil, with high or with low: you must let everything come to pass, and remain free to exercise your love and to satisfy Him whom in Love you love. This is really what you owe, if you live truly, to God and to all men who live with you in Him: to love God singly and solely, and to give your heart to nothing else than to that Love which has chosen you for itself.

And now understand what is the essence of your soul, understand what is meant by 'soul'. 'Soul' is a life which is perceived through God, and which perceives God Himself. And 'soul' is a life which longs to be sufficient to God, which in all it does and all it leaves undone preserves its excellence, so long as it never stoops to anything alien or inferior to the honour of the soul. When the soul preserves its excellence, it is an abyss in which God is sufficient to Himself, in which always He tastes the joy which He has in Himself and which the soul has in Him. 'Soul' is the road on which God travels from His depths into His freedom, and God is the road the soul travels into its freedom, that is, into its depths, which cannot be attained except by sinking down deep. And so long as God does not belong in His totality to the soul, He cannot be enough to it.

The faculty of sight which is naturally created in the soul is Charity. Sight has two eyes, which are Love and Reason. Reason can only see God in what He is not, Love will never rest till it attains to what He is. Reason has its safe highways along which it progresses. Love feels itself impotent, but its impotence brings it further than Reason. Reason attains to God by means of that which is not God. Love is indifferent to what is not God, and is glad that it is impotent when it sees the power of God. Reason has more satisfaction than Love, but Love has more sweet blessedness than Reason. And yet these two are of very great service one to the other, for it is Reason which instructs Love, and Love illumines Reason. And when Reason yields to the desires of Love, and Love is constrained and bound by Reason's prescriptions, then together they are capable of great things. Yet this is something which no one can learn except through experience. For wisdom has no part in this, in the exploring of those marvellous unfathomable depths, hidden to all human knowledge, to which the soul is constrained by Love and which it can only know in the delight of Love. In this joy no one can have a part who is without Love, nor can any stranger share it, but only that soul which is suckled at the breast of the boundless joy of our great Love, which is chastized by Love's fatherly rod, which cleaves inseparably to God, which reads its sentence in His countenance, and then remains in peace.

But when this exalted soul returns to men and to human affairs, its countenance is then so joyful, so wonderfully sweet with the oil of charity, that it turns to men in loving kindness to do all for them that Charity would have. But through the truth and the justice of the judgments which it has read in the countenance of God it appears to men who are not yet exalted as though tremendous and terrifying. And when such men then see that the soul is all armed with truth, equipped in all the ways of truth, how terrifying and tremendous is the soul then! All men must yield to it, under the constraint of Love. And those who have been chosen for this exalted union with Love but who are not yet of sufficient stature for it, already they possess eternal power in their grasp, yet they and others do not know this yet.

So it is that Reason illumines in secret; and when the soul sees, it is illumined in all the truths of God's will. For whoever reads his sentence in the countenance of God acts in all his works in perfect obedience of Love's laws. To be obedient to the law of Love is to contend against the customs of many earthly men. Such a man must not do as everyone else does, he must act in obedience to the truths of omnipotent Love, for it is in truth that Love preserves its commands. He is subject to no one except to Love alone, and Love holds him captive in Love. Whatever anyone else may wish him to say, he speaks according to the will of Love. And he serves and performs the works of Love according to Love's will, night and day, in perfect freedom, never hesitating, never fearing, never grudging, according to the judgments which he has read in Love's countenance, and which remain hidden from those who renounce the works of Love for earthly reasons and for earthly affairs, lest they suffer the contempt of earthly men. They would rather do their own will than the will of Love; they have not yet attained to the sight of that omnipotent Love, in which man can live free amid every kind of oppression.

You can know this freedom, and you can know those who serve in it. Men judge everything by themselves; and so they despise the works of Love, because they think that they can have a greater freedom, or because they think Love's service imprudent. Some devise rules of their own to ensure that Love's rule be neglected. But those choice souls who will keep the rule of Love according to the teachings of illumined Reason, they ignore the commands and the counsels of those who are strangers to Love, whatever sufferings may come to them through this, reproaches, slander, complaints, threats, contempt, imprisonment, homelessness, nakedness, and total destitution. All this is indifferent to them, whether they enjoy a good reputation or a bad; always they stand ready to do Love's bidding, in everything which Love may want, and they dedicate themselves in truth to Love, they endure every suffering with joyful hearts, filled with the power of Love.

So with your whole being you must contemplate God, never turning away from Him the sweet eyes of your longing to be one with Him, a longing always turning to the Beloved for its delight. This means that you must contemplate God with such devotion, and with so much more than devotion, that the eyes of your longing to be one with Him never leave the countenance of your Beloved, pierced with the nails of a burning longing which is never stilled. Then at last you may rest with St John, who slept upon Jesus' breast. And so do those today who in freedom serve Love; they rest upon the sweet and holy breast of Jesus, and they see and hear secret words, unutterable and inaudible to men, the words spoken to them in the sweet whisperings of the Holy Spirit.

So you must constantly contemplate that Beloved whom you desire; for whoever gazes upon what he desires will be set all on fire, so that his heart within him fails under the sweet burden of Love. And as he perseveres in this holy life of contemplation in which we set all our gaze upon God, he is drawn into God, so that Love always makes him to taste its sweetness, and he renounces everything that is upon earth, and he determines, whatever Love's enemies may do to him, that he will rather deny himself a hundred thousand times than that he will fail in the smallest observance in his service of that true Love which is founded upon Christ.

LETTER 19

May God be with you, and give you as your prize
To look upon the ways of Love with seeing eyes,
And give you knowledge what true Love may be:
'I love my true Love, my true Love loves me.'
So in the Song of Songs the Bride has said.
If we by true Love would be conquered
We then could wholly conquer Love so true.
I hope that this may come to pass for you.
Though we grow weary, waiting for that day,
Still all our thanks to true Love we must pay.
Whoever longs to taste how Love is sweet,
Sweet when we search for it, sweet too when we meet,
For him there is no straight and easy road,
A weary traveller urged on by Love's goad,
Up the steep hillside, down into darkest vale,
In torment and in longing where all comforts fail,
Wandering strange unknown to human kind

As Love's great steed drags him along behind.
For never could mere reason once believe
How Love in Love the loved one does perceive,
And how in all things Love lives free.
When to this freedom then the soul attained be,
This freedom which true Love alone can give,
It cares no more whether it die or live.
It longs for Love alone: nothing less can avail.
And here I leave my rhymes, for here my senses fail.

For there are no ideas through which one can express what is that Love which I wish and long for you to have. I will say nothing more: now one must speak not with the tongue but with the soul. Our material is too great; for we have taken as our theme Love, which God Himself by nature is. True Love is no material thing, true Love is beyond matter, immeasurable in God's great freedom, giving always from its superabundance, working always in its ability, always growing in its nobility.

Oh, if only you could grow to the full estate of honour to which you have been called by God from all eternity! How can you endure it, that God in His nature takes delight in you, yet you take no delight in Him? What I myself know of this matter, of that I must be silent. Read what you have written for you; and then please to let me keep silence. Let God do as pleases Him. I can say as Jeremias says: 'O, Lord, You have deceived me, but gladly will I be deceived by You.'

The soul which is most unattainable is the soul most like to God. Preserve yourself, unattainable, from all created beings in heaven and upon earth, until that day when God 'is lifted up from the earth, and draws you and all things to Himself'. Some say that in these words of the Scriptures He means the Cross upon which He was lifted up; but when God and the blessed soul are one, then is He best and most perfectly lifted up from the earth with the blessed soul. For when nothing remains to the soul but God, when the soul preserves no will of its own but lives only according to God's will alone, losing itself and wanting nothing but what is God's will, wholly absorbed and brought to nothing in Him, then God is perfectly lifted up from the earth, and He draws all things to Himself, and so the soul becomes perfectly that which He is.

The souls absorbed into God, who are thus lost in Him, are illumined on the one side by the light of Love, just as the moon receives its light from the sun. And from this new light they also obtain a singular knowledge, from which they proceed and in which they dwell, and so their other side is also given a singular light, and so the two halves of the soul become one, and then it is completed.

If you had waited for this light for the sake of your Beloved, it would have set you free. For those who live in the light are united and clothed in that incomparable light with which God clothes Himself.

For the two halves of the soul to become one, much is needed to achieve this, and I dare not say more about it. For I myself am not sufficiently advanced in Love, and, furthermore, strangers would sow here nettles, where roses ought to grow. Let us say no more of this now. God is with you.

LETTER 20

The nature from which true Love proceeds has twelve hours, which drive Love out of itself and back into itself again. And as Love then returns into itself, it draws in with it all that for the sake of which the unnameable hours had driven it out of itself: a searching mind, a longing heart and a loving soul. And when Love brings these within itself, it hurls them into the abyss of that mighty nature in which Love is born and fed. Then the unnameable hours enter into the unknown nature, and so Love has returned to itself and rejoices in its own nature, beneath it, above it and all around it. And all those who have not attained to this experience take offence at those who have known it, who can act and live and die accordingly, as they are commanded by Love and Love's nature.

At the first unnameable hour of the twelve which draw the soul into the nature of Love, Love reveals itself, and touches the soul, unexpected, uninvited.

At the second unnameable hour Love causes the lover's heart to taste a mighty death, and Love causes the soul to die without its knowing how to die, and even though it has known Love

At the third unnameable hour, Love teaches how a man can die and live in Love, and reveals that no one can love without great sorrows.

At the fourth unnameable hour, Love lets the soul savour Love's hidden judgements, deeper and darker than any abyss. Then Love lets the soul know how wretched man is without Love. Yet still the soul does not know what is the life of Love. This is called truly an unnameable hour; for man must accept the judgements of Love before he has any experience of Love itself.

At the fifth unnameable hour Love entices the soul and the heart, and makes them travel, up out of themselves and out of the nature of Love, and back again into the nature of Love. And then the soul loses its amazement over the power of Love, God's judgments are to it no longer dark, and Love's torments pass away. And then the soul can experience Love in no other way than in Love itself. This seems a decline, but it is not. So it may well be called an unnameable hour: since then, when one is so close to knowing, one is poorer in knowledge than ever before.

At the sixth unnameable hour Love lets it be seen that Love scorns Reason and all that lies in Reason and above it and below it. Whatever belongs to reason is all in conflict with the whole some and just nature of Love. For it is not in the power of Reason to give to Love, to take away from Love. For the true law of Love is a great river, ever increasing, never resting, never stopping.

At the seventh unnameable hour the soul learns that nothing can remain in Love, that nothing can touch Love except desire. And the most secret depths of Love's being are this touching of its being. And this touching springs from Love itself. For Love constantly longs for itself and consumes itself. And Love is still in itself whole and perfect. Love can remain in everything. Love can remain in Charity, but Charity cannot remain in Love. In Love there can remain no pity, no grace, no humility, no reason, no fear, no husbandry, no moderation, nothing. Yet Love remains in all these, and they are all nourished by Love But Love itself receives no morsel, but feeds only upon its own perfection.

At the eighth unnameable hour the soul recognizes that Love's nature in its countenance is the most marvellous thing of all to know. Commonly it is the countenance which shows most clearly the nature of the being; but in Love it is this which is most hidden. For this is Love, itself in itself; and its other limbs, and its acts, are easier to recognize and to understand.

At the ninth unnameable hour the soul learns that when Love attacks most violently, approaches most cruelly, pierces most deeply, then does Love's countenance shine out most sweetly, most peaceably, most loveably, and then Love proffers itself most lovingly. And the more deeply it wounds the one whom it attacks, the more sweetly does it absorb the beloved into itself in the splendour of its countenance.

At the tenth unnameable hour the soul learns that Love is called to account by no one, but that everyone is called to account by Love. Love gains from God the power to judge over those whom it loves. Love does not abase itself before saints or men, not before angels, not before heaven or earth. Love holds God's divinity captive within its nature. Love calls in all the hearts of all who love with a loud voice, never silent, never ceasing: 'Love Love.' This voice is of great compass, it can strike terror as the thunder. These words are the bonds in which Love binds its captives, they are the sword with which it pierces its wounded. They are the rod with which Love chastizes its children, they are the master-trade it teaches its apprentices.

At the eleventh unnameable hour Love holds those whom it loves in its power by force, so that for no single instant can their minds wander nor their hearts long nor their souls love. Love so holds their memories fast that they cannot think of saint or of man, of heaven or earth, not of angels, not of themselves, not of God, but only of the Love which has possessed them and possesses them more and more.

At the twelfth unnameable hour the soul in the very heights of its nature grows like to Love. Now at last Love issues out of itself, and acts with itself, and then sinks back into itself again; for Love finds its whole satisfaction in its own nature. So Love is sufficient to itself: even if no one were to love Love, its own name would be sufficient to gratify its own loveable and noble nature. Its name is its being within it; and its name is its deeds outside it; and its name is its crown above it; and its name is its ground beneath it.

There are the twelve unnameable hours of Love. For in no single one of these twelve hours can anyone understand the Love of Love, except for those, as I said, who are cast into the abyss of the mighty nature of Love, or who are intended for this. And these last are those who believe the more as they understand the more about it.

Blessed John Ruysbroek

THE BOOK OF THE SPARKLING STONE

The man who wishes to live most perfectly according to Holy Church's precepts must be a zealously good man, and a devoutly spiritual man, and an exaltedly contemplative man, and a man directed wholly away from himself towards God and all His creatures. When these four qualities are present in one man, then is his life perfect, and yet still growing and increasing in graces, in all virtues, and in knowledge of truth; and so he will appear before God and all rational beings.

PART I

Now notice three qualities which make a good man. The first quality which a good man must possess is a pure conscience, free from every accusation of mortal sin; and therefore any man who wants to be good must examine and observe with great strictness his whole life from the time when he was first capable of committing sin. And he must cleanse himself of sins committed since that time, according to the law and the custom of Holy Church. The second quality which a good man must possess is that he must be obedient in all things to God and to Holy Church and to his own discretion. If he observes this threefold obedience, he will live free from doubt and sorrow, and within himself he will know that his life is blameless. The third quality which every man must possess is that God's glory must be his chief intention in all his deeds. But even though he does not always have God before his eyes, because he has so many distracting things to do, at the very least he must do them with the intention and the wish to live according to God's dearest will. Here are the three qualities which, when he possesses them, make a man good, and if he lacks one of them he is not good, nor is he in God's grace. But when once a man has resolved in his heart to perfect in himself these three qualities, however evil he may have been till now, in that same instant he becomes a good man, and acceptable to God, and filled with His grace.

Yet if this man who is now good is to become a devoutly spiritual man, three further qualities are needed. The first quality is a heart given solely to God. The second quality is a spirit free from desires. The third quality is to feel an inward unity with God. And now let every man who thinks himself spiritual look closely at himself. If anyone wants to give his heart solely to God, he must have no love for his possessions, no wilful clinging or turning to other men. For all such turning to men and all love which is not purely directed to God's glory deforms man's heart, for such love is born not of God but of the flesh. And therefore, if man is to become spiritual, he must deny all fleshly loves, clinging with joy and love to God alone and so possessing Him. If he does so, all such distractions of his heart, all inordinate love of creatures will be driven out; and in the loving possessing of God man is inwardly shaped in His image, for He is a spirit whom no one can misshape. The second quality is an inner freedom, which comes when man can raise himself, undivided and unimpeded, to God in his every spiritual exercise: giving Him thanks, telling His praises, paying honour to Him, praying to Him with devotion, loving Him dearly, in everything which with the help of God's grace and a zealous spirit can bring us delight and love in our spiritual exercises. And it is through these exercises that we attain to the third quality, when we feel a spiritual unity with God. The man who in his spiritual exercises can climb, undistracted and unimpeded, towards his God, and whose intention is only God's glory, he can taste the goodness of God, and in himself can feel true union with God. And in this union an interior spiritual life is perfected; for out of this union man's longings are stirred and awakened again to fresh works of the spirit, and so the spirit mounts in its works to a fresh union, and so its works and its union with God are constantly renewed. And this renewal in works and in union, this is a spiritual life. And in this way you can see for yourselves that a man becomes good by virtuous practices and right intention, and becomes spiritual by interior virtues and union with God; and without these qualities he can be neither good nor spiritual.

But still you must know that if this spiritual man is to become contemplative, to see God, three more qualities are needed. The first quality is that he feel the foundation of his being to be un-fathomable; and so he must preserve it. The second quality is that his exercises must be without manner. The third quality: his indwelling must be a divine delectation. Understand this, you who wish to live in the spirit, for I am talking to no-one but you. The union with God which a spiritual man experiences, in the bound-less revelation which is granted to him in spirit, is immeasurably deep, immeasurably high, immeasurably far and wide. In this same revelation the spirit knows that through love it has sunk away from itself into the depths, has been lifted up into the heights, has gone far off into the distance. The spirit feels itself to be straying far away, to be dwelling in an unknown place which it yet knows, and, when it feels a loving uniting, that it has been borne along into unity, and that now, dying, it has come to that living which is God. And there it feels that it is one life with God. And this is the foundation and the first quality of contemplative life.

And out of it there grows the second quality, an exercise above reason and without manner; for this union with God, which every contemplative spirit has possessed in love, constantly draws and urges the divine Persons and all loving spirits into the spirit itself. And every man who loves feels this drawing-in, deeply, perhaps, or a little, according to the measure of his love and the manner of his exercise. And whoever knows this drawing-in and does not lose it cannot fall into mortal sin. But a contemplative man, who has renounced himself and all things, who feels no drawing-back from this, because he possesses nothing he would call his own, but stands emptied of all things, he is able to come, naked and unhindered, into the depths of his spirit. There he will find reveal-

93

ed an everlasting light, and in this light he experiences the everlasting admonition of the unity of God. And he feels himself to be an everlasting flame, that burns with a desire beyond all desires to be one with God. And as he comes to know this drawing-in and this admonition better, he feels it more, and as he feels it more he longs more to be one with God, for he longs to pay this debt which God requires of him. God's unity is constantly made known to him, and this makes an everlasting burning of love in his spirit. But as the spirit never ceases to pay this debt, this causes in him an everlasting burning-away; for as in unity all spirits are formed above themselves, they die to their own works, and feel nothing but that they are all consumed in the simple unity of God. No one can feel or possess this simple unity of God unless he stand before Him in an immeasurable clarity, in a love beyond reason and without manner. And standing so, the spirit feels in itself an everlasting burning in love, and in this fire of love it finds neither end nor beginning, and it feels itself to be one with this fire of love.

So the spirit remains, ever burning within itself, for its love is everlasting, and it feels itself everlastingly consumed in love's fire, for it is drawn in and formed again in the unity of God. When the spirit burns in love, if it regards itself it finds distinctions and differences between itself and God, but when it has been consumed it is simple, has nothing to distinguish it, and so feels nothing else than unity with God. For the immeasurable flame of the love of God devours and consumes every thing upon which it seizes. And so you may see that this drawing-in of the unity of God is nothing else but the immeasurable love which draws in the Father and the Son and all that has life in Them into an everlasting delectation. And it is in this love that we long to burn and to be consumed without end in eternity; for it is in this that the blessedness of all spirits reposes. If to this end we will build all our lives upon an unfathomable abyss, we shall constantly sink, down into love and away from ourselves, into the immeasurable depths. And with this same love we shall rise above ourselves into incomprehensible heights; and we shall be lost in this love that has no manner, and this love will lead us safe into the measureless vastness which is God's love. And in that love we shall be borne along, away from ourselves, into the wealth beyond telling of the riches and goodness of God. There we shall melt and vanish, revolve and decline in the glory of God. In each of these analogies I am explaining to contemplative men what they are and what they do; but no one else will understand it, because contemplative life cannot be taught to others. But when eternal truth is revealed to them in the spirit, then all things which are needful will be taught to them.

PART 2

Therefore the Spirit of the Lord says, in the Book of Divine Revelation which St John wrote: 'To those who conquer,' He says—that is, to those who conquer and subdue themselves and all things—'I shall give,' He says, 'the hidden bread of heaven'— that is an inward, hidden delight and a heavenly joy— 'and I shall give them,' He says, ' a sparkling stone, and in this stone a new name written, which no man knows but he who receives it.' This stone is called *calculus*, a pebble under the heel, because it is so small that even if men tread on it they are not hurt; and it is of a shining clarity, and it is red as a flame of fire, and it is small and round and smooth and light.

This sparkling stone signifies for us our Lord Jesus Christ, for through His divinity He is a ray of the everlasting light and a beam of the glory of God, a flawless mirror in which all things live. He who conquers and subdues all things, to him will this sparkling stone be given; and in it he receives light and truth and life. And this stone is also like a flame of fire, for the fiery love of the everlasting Word has filled the whole kingdom of the earth with love, and it wishes to consume all loving spirits in the fire of love. And this pebble is also very small, so that a man will hardly feel it if he tread it under his foot; and that is the reason for its name. This is what St Paul means when he tells us that the Son of God has dispossessed and abased Himself, and has taken on the form of a serf, and has been obedient to the death of the cross. And He says Himself through the prophet's mouth, 'I am a worm and not a man, the scorn of men, rejected by the people.' And in His lifetime he made Himself so small that the Jews trod Him beneath their feet and never felt it; for had they known Him for the Son of God, they had never dared to crucify Him. And still He is small and unheeded in the hearts of all men who do not love Him.

This precious stone of which I speak is round, and equal in all its parts. The roundness of the stone teaches us that divine truth has neither beginning nor end. Its smoothness and equality everywhere teach us that He will weigh all things equally, and give to every man according to his deserts, and what He gives will be an eternal gift. The last property of this stone of which I will speak is that it is exceptionally light; for the everlasting Word of the Father has no weight, and yet in its power it bears up heaven and earth. And it is equally close to all things, and yet no one can follow it, for it goes above and before all creatures, and it will only reveal itself to whom it will and where it will. And it is by its lightness that our heavy humanity has mounted beyond all the heavens, and sits crowned at the right hand of its Father.

Here is the sparkling stone which is given to the contemplative man, and in this stone there is a new name written, which no one knows but he who receives it. You must know that all spirits are named when they turn again to God, each one apart according to the excellence of his service and the depth of his love, but this is only the first name of innocence which we received in baptism, which has been adorned with the merits of our Lord. And when through sin we lose this name of innocence, if still we will be obedient to God, and especially in the three works which He wishes to work in us, we shall be baptized again in the Holy Spirit, and there we shall receive a new name which remains ours for ever.

Now see what are our Lord's three works which He performs in all men who will work with Him to that end. The first work which God performs for all men alike is that He calls them all alike and bids them to union with Him. And as long as the sinner is deaf to this call, he is bound to lack all the other gifts of God which ought to follow this.

Now I have seen that all sinners are divided into five categories. The first is all those who are heedless of good works, who want to live for bodily ease and sensual pleasure, taken up with the world's affairs and the longings of their divided hearts. Such men are incapable of receiving God's grace; and even if they did receive it, they could not retain it. The second category is those who have willingly and knowingly fallen into mortal sin, and who yet perform good deeds, and always they fear God and dread Him, and love good men and ask for their prayers and put their trust in them. Yet as long as they turn back again to their sins and take delight in them, this will weaken and defeat in them that love for God which would turn them to Him, and so they are always unfit to receive His grace. The third category of sinners are all those in whom faith is lacking or erroneous. For however good the works may be which they perform, however excellent their conduct, still without faith they cannot be pleasing to God; for true faith is a foundation of all holiness and of all virtue. The fourth category is those who persist in mortal sin, fearless and shameless, despising God and His gifts and heedless of virtue, considering all spiritual life to be so much hypocrisy or delusion. Whatever people may say to them about God or virtue they listen to under compulsion, for their own minds are made up as if there were no God, nor heaven nor hell. They want to know of nothing but what they can feel and have at this moment. Know that these people are all rejected and despised by God, because they sin in the Holy Spirit. Yet even they can turn again, but that happens only seldom, and with difficulty. The fifth category of sinners are those hypocrites who perform good exterior works, not for God's glory or for their own blessedness, but to gain the name of saints or for some other transient thing. Outwardly they seem to be good and holy, but within they are false and turned away from God, lacking His grace and every virtue.

So I have described for you five categories of sinners. All of them are called to union with God, but as long as such sinners will spend themselves in the service of sin they remain deaf and blind, incapable of tasting or feeling all the good which God wants to perform in them. But when once the sinner comes to himself and sees what he is, if then he hates his sinful life, so he draws near to God; and if he then wants to obey God's call and command, he must at once begin to forsake his sins and to do penance. So he becomes submissive to God and of one mind with Him, and so he receives His grace.

And therefore the first thing which we must see is that God in His free goodness calls and commands to union with Him all men, without distinction, both good and bad, leaving no one out. Secondly, we must feel the goodness of God, which flows out in grace to all men who are obedient to His call. Thirdly, we must clearly perceive and understand that we are able to become one with God in life and spirit, if we will deny ourselves in every way, and follow God's grace up to that highest place where it will lead us; for the operation of God's grace follows the same order in every man, according to the measure and the manner in which he will receive it. This is why, through the common working of the grace of God, every sinner receives the wisdom and strength to forsake sin and turn to virtue, if only he wishes. And through the secret co-operation of the grace of God, every good man can conquer all sins and resist all temptations and perfect all virtues and attain to the highest perfection, if only he is obedient in all things to the grace of God. For everything which we are, and everything which we have received, from without and from within, all is of God's free gift, for which we ought to thank Him and with which we must serve Him, if we are to be acceptable to Him. But there are many of God's gifts which to good men are helps and occasions to virtues, and to evil men helps and occasions to sins, such as health and beauty and wisdom, riches and worldly esteem. These are God's meanest, least precious gifts, which He gives alike for the use of His friends and His enemies, to the evil and to the good. And with them good men serve God and His friends, and the evil serve their flesh and the devil and the world.

See, too, how such men accept God's gifts as His hirelings, and the others as His faithful servants. And they are unlike each other in all their interior works, in their love and their intention, their feelings, in their interior works and their outward exercises. Take note of this: all men who love themselves so inordinately that they will not serve God except for their own profit and their own reward, they all separate themselves from God, and hold themselves captive in their own self-love, for in everything they do, they seek and intend only themselves. So in all their prayer and in all their good works they are seeking the things of this world, or, it may be, everlasting things, which yet they choose for their repute or for their own profit. Such men are inordinately concerned with themselves, and that is why they are always alone in themselves, for they lack that true love which should unite them with God and with all His loved ones. And though these men may seem to keep God's law and commandments, they do not keep the law of love. Whatever they do, it is done under compulsion and not in love, merely to escape damnation. Because inside themselves they are untrustworthy, they dare not put their trust in God, and all their inward life is passed in doubt and fear, toil and misery. On the right they can see that everlasting life which they are afraid of losing; and on the left they can see those everlasting torments of hell which they are afraid of incurring. All the prayer and the effort and the good works which they can perform to drive away this fear are of no avail; the more inordinate is their self-love, the more their eyes are turned in dread towards hell. And from this you can see that their fear of hell comes from their own self-love.

The prophet and the Book of Wisdom say, 'The beginning of wisdom is the fear of God.' But this fear we feel when we look to the right, and see our everlasting blessedness which we may lose. Such fear comes from every man's natural inclination towards blessedness, which is to see God. That is why, even though a man may be unfaithful to God, if he will look into himself he will feel that he is directed from himself towards the blessedness which is God. And such men fear to lose this blessedness, because they love themselves more than God; and their love of blessedness is a perverse love, a self-love. Yet we are told that the fear of the Lord is the beginning of wisdom, and this is law also for the faithless servants of God, for it compels man to forsake sin and to desire virtue and to perform good works, and so he is prepared from without to receive the grace of God and to become a faithful servant. But in that very moment in which he with God's help is able to conquer his self-love, that is when he becomes so free of self that he can trust in God for everything which he needs, as he does this he becomes so acceptable to God that He gives him His grace; and by means of this grace he feels a true love, and love drives out doubt and fear, and makes him to trust and to hope. And so he becomes a faithful servant, and comes to love and intend God in all that he does. And here you have the difference between faithful and faithless servants.

Yet we can see a great difference between God's faithful servants and His secret friends. For through God's help and grace, faithful servants choose to keep His commandments, that is to be obedient to God and to Holy Church in all kinds of virtues and pious practices. And this is called exterior life, or outward life. But God's secret friends choose to keep not only His commandments but His living word, that is a loving inward cleaving to God for His everlasting glory, and a willing denial of everything which one could have delight or love for, except God alone. God calls and commands all such friends to come within, and He teaches them discretion in their interior exercises, and many of the secrets of spiritual life. But He sends His servants out, so that they may faithfully serve Him and His family in all that they do and in every kind of good exterior works.

You can see from this that God gives His grace and His help according to each man's capacity, that is according to each man's submissiveness to Him, either in good exterior works or in good interior exercises of love. But no one can use or feel interior exercises unless he be wholly and utterly turned inward to God; for as long as a man's heart is divided, his eyes are turned outside himself, his disposition is unsettled, and he is easily moved by the joys and the sorrows of the world, for the world still lives in him. Though he may conform to God's commandments, inside himself he is still without light or teaching; for the inward exercises are unknown to him, and how one should practise them. But because he knows and feels that he wants God and longs to accomplish His dearest will in all his works, he lets himself be satisfied with this, because it seems to him that his intention is pure and his service faithful. With such purity and such fidelity he is satisfied, and it seems to him that good exterior works, performed with a right intention, are more holy and fruitful than interior exercises, because he through God's help has chosen an exterior manner of life. And so he pays more heed to the exterior works which he performs than to Him for whom with inward love he performs them; and that is why he is occupied more with what he does than with God for whom he does it.

And it is because of this preoccupation with works that he remains an exterior man, and is not able to fulfil the counsels of God. For his exercises are more outward than inward, more of the senses than of the spirit. And even though he is a faithful servant of our Lord in his outward service, that which the secret friends of God experience remains to him hidden and unknown. And this is why this very man, crude as he is and taken up with outward things, is always judging and finding fault with inward men, because it seems to him that they are lazy. This was why Martha complained to our Lord about her sister Mary, because she did not help her with the work; for it seemed to Martha that she was working hard and being useful, and that her sister sat there doing nothing and wasting time. But our Lord pronounced sentence and judgment on them both. He did not blame Martha for working, because her work was useful and good; but He did blame her for being so preoccupied, and because she was so weighed down and troubled by her many outward works. And He praised Mary for her interior exercises, and He said that only one thing was necessary, and that she had chosen the best part, and that it would not be taken away from her.

This one thing which is necessary to all men is divine love. The best part is an interior life, with a loving cleaving to God. That was what Mary Magdalen chose, and that is what our Lord's secret friends still choose. But Martha chose a purely outward active life, and that is the other part in which men serve God, but it is not so perfect or so good. And this is the part which faithful servants still choose for the love of our Lord. But nowadays we find men so obstinate that they want to be so inward and so unoccupied that they refuse to work and help the needs of their fellow Christians. You may be sure that such men are neither our Lord's secret friends nor yet His faithful servants, for they are altogether false and deceived, because no one can suffice the word of God who will not keep His commandments. And this is why our Lord's secret friends are always His faithful servants too when there is need. But the faithful servants are not all secret friends, because they know nothing of the exercises which are needful for this. And so you can see the difference between the secret friends and the faithful servants of our Lord.

Yet there is still a higher and finer distinction, and that is between the secret friends and the hidden sons of God. Both of them alike stand upright in the presence of God; but His friends have attachment to the interior life, for they choose a loving cleaving to God as the best and the highest which they can attain or desire. Because of this, they cannot pass beyond themselves and their works into bareness and freedom from all attachment; for self remains for them a necessary means, and they are concerned with themselves and with their work. And even though as they cleave to God in love they may experience union with Him, still in that union they always perceive distinction and difference between themselves and Him. For that simple passing-over into a state of bareness which has no manner, that they neither know nor love. And so their highest interior life remains a thing of reason and manner. And though they may have clear understanding and perception of all rational virtues, what it is to gaze, simply and with no mental effort, into the divine clarity, this remains hidden from them. Though they may feel themselves drawn up to God in the powerful fire of love, they do not lose themselves, they are not destroyed and consumed in the unity of love. Though they may wish to live always in God's service and to be everlastingly acceptable to Him, they do not wish to die in Him to all individuality of spirit and to live only a life one with His life. Though they may set little store by the consolations and the repose which come from without, they set great store by God's gifts and their interior works, and the consolations and favours which within themselves they feel. So they sit down to rest by the road; they do not die to everything else so that they may gain the greatest prize, a love that is bare and without manner. Though they may practise and seek a loving cleaving to God, and climb along the inward, upward path that leads to His presence, still there remain hidden from them and unknown that passing-over which is without manner, that blind wandering which is so rewarding, into a love beyond being in which no one can find end or beginning, manner or form.

And this is why there is such difference between God's secret friends and His hidden sons. For the friends experience nothing in themselves except a loving, living ascent towards God which has manner; but the sons go beyond this, to experience a simple, dying passing-over which has no manner. The interior life of our Lord's friends is in exercise, is in a climbing in love, and this they will not give up because they feel attachment to it; but they have no experience of how God is possessed, above all exercises, in a naked, empty state of love. But always in true faith they mount towards God, and they wait for Him and for their everlasting blessedness in firm hope, and they cling to Him and are anchored upon Him in perfect love; and so it is well with them, for they are God's delight and He is theirs. Yet they have not attained to an eternal life, for they have not died altogether in God to themselves and to all attachments. But those who remain and persist in their exercises, and in the turning towards God which they have chosen, all these have chosen God for their everlasting portion, and their names and their works have been written from eternity in the living book of His foreknowledge. But those who choose another portion, and in their inward hearts turn away from Him to what is opposed to Him and to sin, and who persist in this, though their names may have been written down and known to God for the earthly works of righteousness which they before performed, because they did not persevere until death, their names will be taken and struck out of the book of life, and they will never taste God or the fruits which come from virtues.

And this is why we all need to examine ourselves with care, and to adorn our inward turning to God with an interior love, and our outward life with good works; and so in hope and joy we may await God's judgement and the coming of our Lord Jesus Christ. But if we could deny ourselves and all attachment to our works, we should then pass beyond all things in the naked, undivided spirit. And in this nakedness we should be worked, without means, by the Spirit of God, and then we should know certainly that we were God's perfect sons; for those who are worked by the Spirit of God are the sons of God, as His apostle says, St Paul. Yet you must know that all goods and faithful men are the sons of God, for they are all born of the Spirit of God, and He lives in them, and He moves and urges each one sparately, according to his capacity, to the virtues and the good works in which they are acceptable to God. But because all men's conversion to God and exercises of love are not alike, I call some His true servants, some His secret friends, and some His hidden sons. Yet they are all servants, friends and sons, for they all serve and love and intend one God, and they all live and work from the free Spirit of God.

And God permits and suffers His friends to do all things which are not contrary to His commandments. For to those who are submissive to His counsel, what He counsels is a command; and therefore no one is disobedient or opposed to God except those who do not keep His commandments. Whatever things God commands or forbids, in the Scriptures or in the law of Holy Church or in our consciences, all those things we must do or shun, or else we are disobedient and we lose God's grace.

But though each day we may fall short, God suffers this, as our reason tells us, because we are unable to prevent this. And such shortcomings do not make us disobedient, because they do not drive away God's grace or our inward peace. Yet always we must deplore all such shortcomings, however petty they may be, and do all that we can to prevent them. And by this I have explained to you what I said at the beginning, that every man must of necessity be obedient in all things to God, to Holy Church and to his own conscience, for I would not wish my words to be a stumbling-block to anyone. And here I can leave what I have said.

But I myself would gladly know how we might become

God's hidden sons, and attain to contemplative life; and this is how it has appeared to me.

As has been said already, we must always live and watch in all virtues, and above all virtues we must die and fall asleep in God. For we must die to sin and be born of God into a virtuous life, and we must deny ourselves and die in God into an eternal life. And so the order of these things will be thus. If we are born of the Spirit of God we are sons of grace, and so all our life will be adorned with virtues, and so we shall conquer everything which is opposed to God; for everything which is born of God conquers the world, says St John. And in this birth all good men are the sons of God. And the Spirit of God impels and moves each one separately to those virtues and those goods work for which he is ready and able. And in this way all are acceptable to God, each one separately, according to the greatness of his love and the excellence of his exercise. But they do not yet feel themselves stable, or that they possess God, nor they are assured of eternal life, for they can still turn back and fall into sin. This is why I call them servants or friends, rather than sons. But if we will raise ourselves up, and if in our ascent towards God we become so singlehearted that pure love is able to seize us in those heights in which she moves above all the exercises of virtues, that is in that source out of which we are born in the spirit, we shall there perish and die in God to ourselves and to every attachment. And in this dying we become the hidden sons of God, and we find in us a new life, and that is an everlasting life. Of these sons St Paul says: 'You are dead, and your life is hidden with Christ in God.'

Now understand that the order of these things is so: as we go towards God, we must carry ourselves and all our works before us as an eternal offering to God, and in God's presence we must leave ourselves and all our works, and, dying in love, we must pass beyond all created things into those riches of God which are beyond being: and there we shall possess God in an eternal death to ourselves. And so the Spirit of God says in the Book of Revelations that the dead are blessed who die in the Lord. Truly he calls them blessed, these dead, for they have died eternally and sunk away from themselves into the delectable unity of God, and they are constantly dying afresh in love as this same unity enters into them and transforms them. And the Spirit of God says furthermore: 'They shall rest from their labour, and their works shall follow them.' In manner, as we are born of God into a spiritual life of virtue, we carry our works before us as on offering to God. But without manner, as we die again in God into an eternal and blessed life, our works follow us, for they are one life with us. As we go towards God with our virtues, God lives in us. But as we pass away from ourselves and from all things, then we live in God. If we have faith and hope and love, we have received God, and He lives in us with His grace. And He sends us out as His faithful servants to keep His commandments, and He calls us back again as His secret friends if we follow His counsel. And so He reveals us plainly as His sons, if we live in opposition to the world. But above all things if we will take delight in God and feel an eternal life in ourselves, we must go in faith, beyond reason, into God.

And in Him we must remain, single, empty, unattached, raised up in love into a sheer emptiness beyond our thoughts. For when in love we pass away from all things, and die to all consciousness, in unknowing and in darkness, there we are worked and transformed by the everlasting Word, which is an image of the Father. And in this empty being of the spirit we receive an incomprehensible clarity, which enfolds and pierces us as the air is pierced by the brightness of the sun. And this clarity is nothing else than a limitless gazing and beholding: what we are we gaze upon, and what we gaze upon we are; for our thought and our life and our being is altogether raised up and inclined to the truth which is God. And therefore in this single beholding we are one life and one spirit with God;

and this I call a contemplative life. When in love we cling to God, then we practise the best part; but when we thus gaze upon Him above being, then we possess Him wholly.

And in so gazing we are using an exercise without manner, we are living a life in which we are annihilated. For when we proceed out of ourselves into darkness, into a state unfathomable and without manner, then always there shines the single ray of the brightness of God, and there we find our foundation, and ir draws us out of ourselves, and we are beyond being and sunk deep in love. And this sinking-down in love must always of necessity lead us on to the exercise, without manner, of love; for love can never be idle, but at all times it longs to see and taste all the immeasurable riches hidden in its depths. This is a hunger that can never be sated: the more it has the more it lacks, and ever it swims against the stream. We cannot leave it, we cannot have it; we cannot forsake it, we cannot attain it; we cannot speak of it nor can we conceal it, for it is beyond reason and understanding, far exalted above all created being. And so it is unattainable and indescribable; but if we look into our innermost selves, there we feel the Spirit of God driving and forcing us in the impatience of love. And we must look above ourselves, and there we feel the Spirit of God drawing us out of ourselves into His being and annihilating us, there, in that love beyond being where we are one with Him, that love we possess more deeply and more fully than any other thing.

And to possess that love so is for us to taste the essence and the depths of every good and of eternal life. And tasting we are swallowed up, above reasoning and without reasoning, in the deep silence of God's nature which can never be disturbed. One can know that this is true by what one feels, and in no other way; for neither reasoning nor experiment will show us how this is, or who, or where, or what. This is why our exercises, as we follow it, will always be without manner. For we cannot comprehend or understand the unfathomable good which we taste and possess; nor will our exercises bring us out of ourselves and into it. And so we are poor in ourselves and rich in God; hungry and thirsty in ourselves, filled with meat and drink in God; active in ourselves, in God empty and idle. And we must always be like this, for without the exercises of love we shall never possess God. Whoever feels or believes that this is not so is deceived.

And so we live wholly in God, in whom we have our blessedness, and wholly in ourselves, where we perform the exercises of love for Him. And even though we do live wholly in God and wholly in ourselves, still this is only one life. To be poor and rich, hungry and filled, active and passive—these things are opposites; and yet our highest excellence, now and in eternity, lies in achieving them. For it is impossible for us both to become God and to lose our created nature; and yet if we remain within ourselves, separated from God, we shall always be outcasts, exiled from blessedness. This is why we must feel ourselves to be wholly in God and wholly in ourselves; and between these two opposites we shall feel and find nothing else than God's grace and the exercise of our love. For it is through what we feel at the highest degree that the brightness of God shines into us, teaching us the truth and moving us to the practice of every virtue and to eternal love for Him whose light we must follow, never ceasing, into the depths from which it proceeds. And in those depths we shall feel nothing else than that we die and sink away into love, single, unfathomable, from which there is no return.

If we could stay there for evermore, never contemplating anything but that, we should never cease to feel it; for when we sink away from ourselves into the depths in which God forms us again, this lasts forever, never ceasing, once we have gone out of ourselves and we possess God, there where we have sunk down into love. For if we possess God there and are lost to ourselves, God is ours and we are His, and we sink away from ourselves forever, without return, into our possession which is God. And this sinking-away is of our essence, and it is done in a love which exalts us; and thus we are so both awake and asleep, whether we are conscious of it or whether we are not. And so this sinking away does not earn for us any greater reward, but it preserves us in the possession of God and of all the riches we have gained. This sinking-away is like the rivers, which never stand still and never turn back, but always flow down to the sea which is their proper place. In the same way, once we possess God alone, in our essence we sink and in love we are raised up, ever flowing, never returning, to that which we possess, which is our own, the depths which we feel. And if we could always remain simple, always contemplate this with the same totality, we should always feel it without any changing.

Now this sinking-away is above every virtue and above every exercise of love, for it is nothing else than an eternal going-out of ourselves, with a clear prevision of a different being, towards which we draw, out of ourselves, as if we already tasted blessedness. For we feel ourselves always drawn out of ourselves into that being different from what our own being is. And this is the innermost difference, the most hidden, which we can feel between ourselves and God, for beyond this there is never any difference.

Yet still our reason lags behind, standing open-eyed in darkness, that is in a profound unknowing. In this darkness the unfathomable brightness will be hidden and concealed from us. For it is unfathomable beyond all conceiving, and so it blinds our reason. But clarity makes us simple in its simplicity, it forms us anew with its own being, and so we are unmade by God and made new when we have sunk away into love, there where we possess our blessedness and are one with God.

When we are so made one with God, there remains a living knowledge of it in us, and a working love, for we cannot possess God without our knowledge, and without the exercise of love we cannot become one or remain one with God. For if we could be blessed without knowing it, a stone, which can know nothing, could be blessed. Supposing that I were the lord of the whole world, what good would it do me if I did not know it? This is why, as we taste and we possess, we must always know and feel. Christ Himself shows this to us, when He says to us of His Father: 'This is eternal life,' He says, 'that they all know that You and He whom You have sent, Jesus Christ, are one true God.' In this you can see that our eternal life consists in knowledge with perception.

I have just said that we are one with God, and that Holy Scripture shows us this. But now let me say that we must to eternity remain something different from God, and that Scripture also shows us this. And we must understand and feel in ourselves both the one and the other, if we are to find truth. This is why I say that the inward vision of our spirit is illumined, beyond the vision of God and beyond our highest feelings, with a brightness which teaches us the truth concerning love and all virtues. And in this brightness we are especially taught four different ways to feel concerning God and ourselves.

In the first place, we feel that God is within us with His graces; and when we perceive that, we cannot be idle. For just as the sun with its light and its heat illumines and gladdens and fructifies the whole world, so God does with His graces: He illumines and He gladdens and He fructifies all men who are willing to be obedient to Him. For if we are to feel God within us, and if the fire of His love is to burn eternally in us, we must of our own free will help Him to stoke the fire, and that in four ways. We must within ourselves remain inwardly united with the fire; and we must go out of ourselves towards all men, with fidelity and brotherly love; and we must go beneath ourselves, in acts of penance and in all good works and in resistance to our immoderate desires; and we must with the flames of this fire go above ourselves in acts of devotion, with thankings and praises and fervent prayer, always persevering in this with a true intention and a heartfelt love. And through this God will dwell in us with His graces; for these four ways comprehend all the exercises which we can use so long as we remain, rational beings, in this life. No one can be pleasing to God without these exercises; and the man who is most perfect in them is closest to God. This is why they are necessary to all men; and only contemplatives can advance beyond them. So we must all begin by feeling that God with His graces is within us, if we want to become His.

Secondly, if we have achieved contemplative life, we must feel that we live in God. And out of this life, in which we feel ourselves in God, a brightness shines upon our inward beholding which illumines our reason and is a means between us and God. And when we stand in this light, our reason illumined, remaining yet within ourselves, still we feel that the very essence of our created life is sinking away into God's eternal life. But when we follow after the light, above reason, with a simple beholding and a willing inclination of ourselves, into our highest life, there we find that the whole self receives a new form from God. And so then we feel ourselves encompassed in God.

And after this we feel a third distinction, which is when we feel ourselves one with God. For through this forming anew by God we feel ourselves to be swallowed up in an unfathomable abyss of our everlasting blessedness, when we are never able to find difference between ourselves and God. There is nothing which we can feel above that, that there is nothing which we can possess except to be sunk down deep in love. So in this way, when we are exalted and moved in our highest feelings, all our powers stand idle, our whole being does nothing but receive God; yet we and our powers are not destroyed, for if so we should lose our created nature. And so long as we can stand idle, our spirits inclined, our eyes open yet not seeing, so long we can contemplate God and receive Him.

But in the very moment in which we want to test and see what it is that we feel, we lapse into reason. And then we find that there is difference and distinction between us and God. And so we find that God is outside us, in incomprehensibility, and that is the fourth of the different ways in which we feel God and ourselves. For here we find ourselves standing in the presence of God; and the truth which we have received from our vision of Him shows us that God wants both to be ours and us to be His. And in this very moment in which we feel that God wants to be ours, a yearning, devouring longing is born in us, so ravening, so deep, so constant that were God to give us all that He has to give, except only Himself, that could never satisfy us. We feel that He has surrendered and given Himself to our free desires, for us to savour Him in every way that we could wish; and then we learn, in the truth of His vision, that all that we savour, compared with what we still lack, is as a drop of water compared with the sea. So in the heat and the impatience of love our spirit is taken by force: the more we taste, the greater our yearning and hunger grow, the tasting increasing our hunger, our hunger making us taste. So we have gained to where we cannot gain what we seek: we feed upon His infinity, with which we cannot nourish ourselves, we have come to His eternity, to which we cannot attain; and so we cannot come into God nor He into us. For in all the impatience of love, we cannot deny our own being: and so its heat is so unbounded that the exercise of love goes and comes between us and God like the lightning in the sky, and still we cannot be consumed in it. In all this storm of love our works are beyond reason and without manner, for love yearns for what it cannot attain. Reason shows that love is right, but reason cannot counsel love or serve it; for as long as we see that God wants to be ours, and our hearts are touched by this, His love stirs our avid desire, and it is from this that comes the impatience of love. For this touching, which comes from God, flows out and kindles our impatience and urges us to act: that is, it makes us to love His everlasting love. But His touching as it pierces us consumes us so that we die to ourselves, it makes us to perish and fail in unity with Him. And when this touching pierces us, we feel that God wants us to be His, because in this we can deny ourselves, and leave Him to accomplish our blessedness. But when He, flowing out to us, touches us, He leaves us to ourselves. He makes us free and sets us in His presence, He teaches us to pray in the Spirit and in freedom to strive towards Him, and He shows to us His incomprehensible riches in as many forms as we can perceive them. For all that we can think of in which consolation and joy repose, all that we find in Him without measure. And therefore when we feel this, that He with all these riches wants to be ours, and always wants to dwell with us, all the powers of our soul yield themselves to this, and especially our yearning desire. For all the rivers of God's graces flow to us; and the more that we taste, the more we long to taste; and the more that we long to taste, the more deeply are we touched by Him; and the more deeply that we are touched by Him, the more does the flood of His sweetness suffuse and submerge us; and the more that we are suffused and submerged, the more clearly do we feel and confess that the sweetness of God is incomprehensible and illimitable. This is why the prophet says: 'Taste and see, for God is sweet.' But he does not say 'how sweet', for His sweetness is beyond measure: and so we cannot comprehend it or consume it. And the bride of God in the Canticles shows us this, and says: 'I have sat in the shadow of Him whom I longed for, and His fruit is sweet to my throat.'

PART 3

There is a great difference between the illumination of the saints, and the highest illumination to which we can attain in this life. For it is the shadow of God which gives light to the desert of our spirit; but upon the high mountain, in the land of the heavens, no shadow is there. And yet it is still the same sun and the same brightness which lightens our desert and the high mountain; but the state of the saints is translucent and glorious, and therefore they receive the light without any means, yet our state is mortal and crude, and this is the means which casts the shadow which overcasts our comprehension, so that we cannot recognize God or any heavenly thing so clearly as do the saints. For as long as we walk in the shadow, we cannot see the sun itself, but our knowledge is 'in similitudes and in mysteries', as St Paul says. Yet the shadow is so illumined by the shining of the sun that we are able to tell true from false, in all the virtues and in all the truth which belong to our mortal existence. But if we could become one with the brightness of the sun, we could then follow love, going out of ourselves and losing our modes of thought and action. It will be when our eyes are blinded that the sun will draw us into its own brightness, when we have union with God. And when we come to feel and understand this about ourselves, we come to that contemplative life which is proper to our state.

The state of the Jews in the Old Law was cold and in night, and their way was set in darkness, and they sat in the shadow of death, as the prophet Isaias says. The shadow of death came from the state of sin which they inherited, and so they all were necessarily separated from God. But our state, in the Christian faith, is still only cool and in the early hours of the day, though the sun has risen for us. So we must walk in the light and sit in the shadow of God, and between us and God His graces must be the means. And by these means we must conquer all things, and die to all things, and pass over, unimpeded, into unity with God. But the state of the saints is hot and bright, for they live and walk in the high noon. And with open, illumined eyes they look upon the sun in its brightness, for they are suffused and submerged in the glory of God. And every man tastes and sees according to the measure of his illumining: this is the fruit of every virtue, as it is gathered in by every spirit. But when they taste and see Trinity in unity and unity in Trinity, when they find themselves united with that, then that is the food beyond compare, and there they drink their fill and in it they find rest.

And it was this that Christ's bride longed for, when she said to him in the Song of Songs: "Show me Him whom my soul loves. Where do You feast, and where do You rest in the noon of the day?" In the noon of the day is in the light of glory, St Bernard says. For every food which is given to us here in the morning hours and in the shade is but a foretaste of the feast which will be ours in the noon of the glory of God. Yet it is the boast of the bride of our Lord that she has sat in the shadow of God and that His fruit is sweet to her throat. When we feel this, that God within us touches us, then we taste of His fruit and His feast, for it is His touching which is His feast. And His touching comes into us and flows out from us, as I said before. When it comes into us, then we can be wholly His: then we learn to die and to contemplate. But when it flows out of us, still He wants to be wholly ours: and then He teaches us to live in the riches of virtues. When His touch penetrates us, all our powers fail, and then we sit in His shadow, and then His fruit is sweet to our throat. For God's fruit is His Son, whom the Father bears in our spirit. This fruit is so immeasurably sweet to our throat that we can consume it or absorb it into us, but it consumes and absorbs us into itself.

And as often as this fruit, coming into us, touches us, we forsake and we conquer all things, and in conquering them we taste that secret bread of Heaven which gives us everlasting life. For we receive the sparkling stone of which I spoke before, in which our new name was written before the world began. This is the new name which no one understands except him who receives it. And everyone who feels himself united with God savours his name according to the manner of his virtues, of his going to God, of his union with Him. And therefore, so that each man may obtain his name and possess it forever, the Lamb of God, that is, our Lord's humanity, has submitted Himself to death and has opened for us the book of life, in which are written all the names of the elect. And of these names not one can be erased, for they are one with that living book which is the Son of God. And it is His death which has broken open for us the seals of the book, so that all virtues may be perfected according to God's everlasting providence. And therefore, so that each man can triumph over himself and die to all things, he feels the penetrating touch of the Father, and the fruit of the Son, born within him, tastes sweet to him; and in this tasting the Holy Spirit makes manifest to him that he is the child and the heir of God. Here are three ways, and no one of them is completely like the others; and this is why each man has his own particular name, and his name is always being made new, through new graces and new deeds of virtue. And therefore all knees bow before the name of Jesus, for He has marched before us and has conquered, and He has brought light to our darkness, and perfected all our virtues in the highest degree. And so His name is exalted above all names, for He is leader and prince above all the elect. And in His name we are called and chosen and adorned with graces and with virtues, and we await the glory of God.

PART 4

And therefore, so that His name may be exalted and illumined in us, we must follow Him up into the mountain of our naked thoughts, just as Peter and James and John followed Him up into the mount of Tabor.

'Tabor' is the same as for us in our language to say 'increase of light'. If we are Peter, 'confessing the truth', and James, 'conquering the world', and John, 'full of grace', possessing virtues and justified before God, then Jesus leads us up into the mountain of our naked thoughts, and reveals Himself to us, glorified in divine brightness. And in His name His heavenly Father opens to us the living book of His eternal wisdom; and God's wisdom enfolds our naked vision and the singleness of our spirit in a savouring, without manner, without multiplicity, without perception of difference, of every good. For there is contemplation and knowledge, tasting and feeling, existing, living, possessing, and being:

and always this is one in our exaltation to God. And it is for this exaltation that we stand and wait, each man in his own way; and our heavenly Father, through His wisdom and His goodness, gives to each man his own gifts, according to the excellence of his life and of his exercise.

So that if we always remained with Jesus up in Tabor, upon the mountain of our naked thought, we should always feel the growth of new light and new truth, for we should always hear the Father's voice, which would touch us, flowing out with graces and coming into us in unity.

All the disciples of our Lord Jesus Christ hear the Father's voice, for He says of them all: 'These are My chosen sons, and they all please Me well.' And as he pleases Him each man receives grace, according to the measure and the manner in which he finds delight in God. And between these two, that God delights us and we delight Him, true love is exercised; and so each man savours his name and his office and the fruits of his exercise. And in this all good men are hidden from those who live for the world, for such are dead to God and nameless, and so they can neither feel nor taste what is proper to the living. This outflowing touching of God makes us living in the spirit, and fills us with graces, and illumines our understanding, and teaches us to know the truth and recognize virtue, and preserves us, as we stand in the presence of God, in such great strength that we are able to sustain all the savour, all the feeling, all the outflowing gifts of God, without our spirit ever failing. But when God's touching pierces us, it urges us on to be one with God, to yield up our spirits and die in blessedness, in that single love which enfolds the Father and the Son in one delight.

And so, when we have climbed with Jesus up the mountain to where we lose perception of all created things, if we then follow Him, looking only upon Him, finding inward delight, inclined in spirit to joy in Him, then we feel the great heat of the Holy Spirit, which makes us burn away and melt in God's unity. For when we, one with God's Son, return again in love to the source of our being, then we hear the Father's voice, piercing and touching us; for He says to all His elect, in His everlasting word: 'This is My dear Son, in whom I made Our delight.' For you must know that the Father with the Son and the Son with the Father have exercised an eternal delight, because the Son was to take upon Himself our humanity, and to die, and to bring back all the elect to their source. And therefore, if we through the Son are exalted to our source, we shall hear the Father's voice, coming into us and illumining us with eternal truth; and the truth will show us God's boundless delight, in which all delights begin and end. It is there that all our powers fail, there that we see clearly and fall prostrate, there that we all become one and single in the loving embrace of the threefold unity. When we feel this unity, we are one being and one life and one blessedness with God, and it is there that all things are made perfect and all things renewed. For there we sink down into the vast embrace of God's love, there is the joy of each man so great and so incomparable that he has neither thought nor eyes for the joy of anyone else. For he is wholly delight and love, that love which itself is all, and he has neither need nor power to seek anything but love.

PART 5

If man is to take delight in God, three things are necessary: true peace, inward silence, a loving cleaving to God. Those who would find true peace between themselves and God must love Him so much that with a free will and for His glory they deny everything which they do or love to excess, which they possess or could possess to God's dishonour. This is the first thing which all men need; and the second, inward silence, is that they must be empty of all things which they ever saw or heard, and not formed in the image of such things. The third thing is a loving cleaving to God; and in that very cleaving is delight. For whoever cleaves to God in pure love, and not for his own profit, truly delights in God, and he feels that he loves God and is loved by Him.

But there are three other things, which are higher, which make men steadfast and capable of delighting in God and feeling Him as He will inspire them to this. The first of these things is to find rest in Him in whom they delight: it is there that love is conquered by love, that love is possessed by love in loving which is naked and essential. There love, loving, falls in love with love, and each is wholly the other's, to possess and to rest in. From this the next thing follows, and that is called a falling asleep in God, for there the spirit sinks down, away from itself, never knowing who or where or how. And from this follows the third thing, and the last of which men can know, which is where the spirit contemplates a darkness which reason cannot penetrate. And there man feels that he has died to himself, that he is lost and that he is one with God, with no perception of difference. And when he feels himself one with God, then God Himself is his peace, his delight and his rest, And so it is an abyss, here where he can die to himself in blessedness, and live again in virtues, as love bids him and prompts him.

Be sure, if you can feel in yourself these six things, you feel everything which I have already said to you, everything which I could ever say. And when you enter upon this state, then contemplation and delight will be as easy and as simple to you as any act of your natural life. And out of these riches comes that common life of which at the beginning I promised you that I would speak.

CONCLUSION

The man whom God sends back again, out of these heights, down into the world, is full of truth and rich in every virtue. And he seeks nothing for himself, but only for the honour of Him who has sent him. So he is just and true in all things, and his being is founded on riches and meekness, and on the riches of God. So he can flow out to all who have need of him; for his treasure is the living well of the Holy Spirit, which no one can exhaust. And he is a living and willing instrument of God, with which God can perform what He wills and how He wills; and for this he takes no credit to himself, but he gives the glory to God. And so he stands always willing and ready to do what God commands; and strong and mighty to suffer and endure all that God lays upon him. And so he lives a common life; for he is ready for either contemplation or action, and in both he is perfect. For no one can have this common life if he is not a contemplative man; and no one can contemplate God or find delight in Him if he has not these six things well ordered in him, as I have said here. This is why all those are deceived who believe that they can live a contemplative life, and yet have inordinate love or use or possession of created things; they think that they have delight in God when they are still formed in the image of His creatures, they believe that they have found rest before they have found delight. For we must be moved to go to God with open hearts, with quiet consciences, looking to Him only, in good faith and perfect truth. Then we shall mount from virtue to virtue, and contemplate God and find delight in Him, and become one in Him, just as I have told you. That this may happen to us all, may God help us. Amen.

BEATRICE

Van dichten comt mi cleine bate.
Die liede raden mi dat ict late
Ende minen sin niet en vertare
Maer om die doghet van hare
Die moeder ende maghet es bleven,
Hebbic een scone mieracle op heven,
Die god sonder twivel toghede
Marien teren, diene soghede.
Ic wille beghinnen van ere nonnen
Een ghedichte, god moet mi onnen,
Dat ic die poente moet wel geraken
Ende een goet ende daer af maken,
Volcomelijc na der waerheide,
Als mi broeder Ghijsbrecht seide,
Een begheven willemijn;
Hi vant in die boeke sijn.
Hi was een out ghedaghet man.
Die nonne, daer ic af began,
Was hovesche ende subtijl van zeden;
Men vint ghene noch heden,
Die haer ghelijct, ic wane,
Van zeden ende van ghedane.
Dat ic prisede haer lede,
Sonderlinghe haer scoonhede,*
Dats een dinc dat niet en dochte.
Ic wille u segghen, van wat ambochte
Si plach te wesen langhen tijt:
Int clooster daer si droech abijt,
Costersse was si daer,
Dat seggic u al over waer:
Sine was lat no traghe,
No bi nachte no bi daghe.
Si was snel te haren werke;
Si plach te ludene in die kerke;

Little profit comes to me from writing poetry, and people advise me to give it up and stop addling my brains. But to the honour of her who remains Mother and Virgin I have undertaken to write of a lovely miracle which God beyond doubt performed to the honour of Mary who suckled Him.

Now I will begin my poem, which is about a nun, and may God grant that I may tell the story properly and make a good end to it, agreeing perfectly with the truth, as Brother Gilbert told it to me, who was a pious Williamite friar. He had found it in his books, and he was a very old man.

This nun, of whom I began to tell you, was well-bred and intelligent: I do not think that one would find anyone today to equal her in breeding and manners. But it would not be seemly for me to extol her, and especially not to speak of her beauty; but I can tell you of the office which for a long time she bore. In the monastery in which she was professed, she was the sacristan, and I can truthfully tell you that she was never slow or lazy, night or day, but she was prompt in her work. She used to ring the church bell,

* The original Dutch text of *Beatrijs* which is printed here, parallel with the English translation, is from *Beatrijs. A Middle Dutch Legend*, edited from the only existing manuscript in the Royal Library at The Hague by A. J. Barnouw (London, Oxford University Press, 1914).

The editor in his Preface to the text remarks: "The use of italics seemed . . . unavoidable in the case of manuscript *oe*, the *e* of which, for the reader's benefit, has been replaced throughout by *o* where ō, not ū is the sound intended".

Si ghereide tlicht ende ornament
Ende dede op staen alt covent.

Dese ioffrouwe en was niet sonder
Der minnen, die groot wonder
Pleecht te werken achter lande.
Bi wilen comter af scande,
Quale, toren, wedermoet;
Bi wilen bliscap ende goet.
Den wisen maect si ooc soo ries
Dat hi moet bliven int verlies,
Eest hem lieft ofte leet.
Si dwingt sulken, dat hine weet
Weder spreken ofte swighen,
Daer hi loon af waent ghecrighen.
Meneghe worpt si onder voet,
Die op staet, alst haer dunct goet.
Minne maect sulken milde,
Die liever sine ghiften hilde,
Dade hijt niet bider minnen rade.
Noch vintmen liede soo ghestade,
Wat si hebben, groot oft clene,
Dat hen die minne gheeft ghemene:
Welde, bliscap ende rouwe;
Selke minne hetic ghetrouwe.
In constu niet gheseggen als,
Hoe vele gheluux ende onghevals
Uter minnen beken ronnen.
Hier omme en darfmen niet veronnen
Der nonnen, dat si niet en conste ontgaen
Der minnen diese hilt ghevaen,
Want die duvel altoos begheert
Den mensche te becorne ende niet en cesseert
Dach ende nacht, spade ende vroe;

she looked after the candles and altar furniture, and she wakened the whole convent.

This virgin did not lead a life without love, love which can perform so many miracles far and wide, love which brings sometimes shame, torment, sorrow, despair, sometimes joy and happiness. Love can make a wise man into such a fool that it brings him to ruin, whether he like it or not. Some love so constrains that they can neither keep silence nor speak, though speech could gain them their reward. When it pleases love, it tramples under foot those who stand upright. Some love makes generous who would withhold all their gifts were it not for the counsels of love. Some are made so steadfast by love that they will share with love whatever they have, much or little, riches, joys or sorrows; and that is what I call true love. I could not tell you of all the good fortune and all the ill which flows out of love's streams. And so we must not blame this nun, who was unable to escape from the love which held her captive; because the devil is always longing to tempt man, and he never stops, day and night, late and early,

Hi doeter sine macht toe.
Met quaden listen, als hi wel conde,
Becordise met vleescheliker sonde,
Die nonne, dat si sterven waende.
Gode bat si ende vermaende,
Dat hise trooste dore sine ghenaden.
Si sprac: 'ic ben soo verladen
Met starker minnen ende ghewont,
Dat weet hi, dient al es cont,
Die niet en es verholen,
Dat mi die crancheit sal doen dolen;
Ic moet leiden een ander leven;
Dit abijt moetic begheven.'

Nu hoort, hoeter na verghinc:
Si sende om den ionghelinc,
Daer si toe hadde grote lieve,
Ootmoedelijc met enen brieve,
Dat hi saen te hare quame,
Daer laghe ane sine vrame.
Die bode ghinc daer de ionghelinc was.
Hi nam den brief ende las,
Die hem sende sijn vriendinne.
Doe was hi blide in sinen sinne;
Hi haestem te comen daer.
Sint dat si out waren .XIJ. iaer,
Dwanc die minne des e twee,
Dat si dogheden menech wee.

Hi reet, soo hi ierst mochte,
Ten clooster, daer hise sochte.
Hi ghinc zitten voor tfensterkijn
Ende soude gheerne, mocht sijn,
Sijn lief spreken ende sien.

and he does all that is in his power. With his evil cunning, which he well knew how to employ, he tempted the nun with sins of the flesh until she longed for death, and she prayed and entreated God to comfort her with His grace. She said: 'I am so oppressed and wounded by my great love that He who knows all things, from whom nothing is hidden, knows that sickness will soon destroy me. I must lead a different life, and I must renounce this habit.'

Now listen to what happened next. She sent for the youth for whom she felt this great love, humbly asking him in a letter to come to her soon, and it would be to his profit. This message reached the young man, who took and read the letter which his mistress had sent him; and then he rejoiced greatly, and hastened to her, for, since they were twelve years old, love had so ruled these two that they had suffered many woes.

As soon as he could he rode to the cloister and sought her out. He sat down in front of the little window, and he longed, if it might be, to speake to his love and see her.

Niet langhe en merde si na dien;
Si quam ende woudene vanden
Vor tfensterkijn, dat met yseren banden
Dwers ende lanx was bevlochten.
Menech werven si versochten,
Daer hi sat buten ende si binnen,
Bevaen met alsoo starker minnen.
Si saten soo een langhe stonde,
Dat ict ghesegghen niet en conde,
Hoe dicke verwandelde hare blye.
'Ay mi,' seitsi, 'aymie,
Vercoren liefm, i es soo wee,
Sprect ieghen mi een wort oft twee,
Dat mi therte conforteert!
Ic ben, die troost ane u begheert!
Der minnen strael stect mi int herte,
Dat ic doghe grote smerte.
In mach nemmermeer verhoghen,
Lief, ghi en hebbet uut ghetoghen!'

Hi antworde met sinne:
'Ghi wet, wel lieve vriendinne,
Dat wi langhe hebben ghedragen
Minne al onsen daghen.
Wi en hadden nye soo vele rusten,
Dat wi ons eens ondercusten.
Vrouwe Venus, die godinne,
Die dit brachte in onsen sinne,
Moete God onse here verdoemen,
Dat si twee soo scone bloemen
Doet vervaluen ende bederven.
Constic wel ane u verwerven,
Ende ghi dabijt wout nederleggen
Ende mi enen sekeren tijt seggen,

She did not long delay after that, but came to discover him at the window, which was latticed with iron bars. They heaved many a deep sigh, as he sat outside and she inside, so imprisoned by their great love. So they sat for a long time, and I could not tell you how often their colour changed. 'Ah me,' she said, 'my beloved, my one true love, I am so full of woe, speak a word or two to me to comfort my heart. I beg you for some consolation. Love's dart has so pierced my heart that I suffer great pain, and unless you can draw it out I shall never be happy again.'

He answered with these words: 'You know, my own dear love, how long we have suffered the pains of love, and yet we have never had the consolation of exchanging one single kiss. God our Lord must surely condemn that goddess, Lady Venus, for making two such lovely flowers fade and die, when she brought this into our minds. If I could persuade you to abandon your habit and to appoint a time

Hoe ic u ute mochte leiden,
Ic woude riden ende ghereiden
Goede cleder diere van wullen
Ende die met bonten doen vullen:
Mantel, roc ende sercoot.
In begheve u te ghere noot.
Met u willic mi aventueren
Lief, leet, tsuete metten sueren.
Nemt te pande mijn trouwe.'
'Vercorne vrient,' sprac die ioncfrouwe,
'Die willic gherne van u ontfaen
Ende met u soo verre gaen,
Dat niemen en sal weten in dit covent
Werwaert dat wi sijn bewent.
Van tavont over .VIIJ. nachte
Comt ende nemt mijns wachte
Daer buten inden vergier,
Onder enen eglentier.
Wacht daer mijns, ic come uut
Ende wille wesen uwe bruut,
Te varen daer ghi begheert;
En si dat mi siecheit deert
Ocht saken, die mi sijn te swaer,
Ic come sekerlike daer,
Ende ic begheert van u sere,
Dat ghi daer comt, lieve ionchere.'

Dit gheloofde elc anderen.
Hi nam orlof ende ghinc wanderen
Daer sijn rosside ghesadelt stoet.
Hi satter op metter spoet
Ende reet wech sinen telt
Ter stat wert, over een velt.
Sijns lieves hi niet en vergat.

when it would be safe to lead you out of here, then I would ride off and obtain fine woollen clothes and have them lined with fur, cloak and gown and jacket. I would not desert you in any need: I will risk with you whatever may be our lot, joy or sorrow, sweet or sour; and receive my promise as a gage.' 'My dearest love,' the virgin said, 'I am glad to accept your promise, and I shall go away with you so far that no one in this convent shall know what has become of us. Tomorrow week, at night, come here and wait for me outside in the orchard under the eglantine. Wait for me there; I shall escape and I will be your bride, to travel with you wherever you like. Unless sickness prevents me, or circumstances too strong for me, I shall certainly come, and I beg you to be there also, my dear lord.'

So either believed the other's promise, and he took his leave and went off to where his steed stood saddled. He mounted it in speed and galloped off across the land towards the town. He did not forget what he had promised his love,

Sanders daghes ghinc hi in die stat;
Hi cochte blau ende scaerlaken,
Daer hi af dede maken
Mantele ende caproen groot
Ende roc ende sorcoot
Ende na recht ghevoedert wel.
Niemen en sach beter vel
Onder vrouwen cledere draghen.
Si prysdent alle diet saghen.
Messe, gordele ende almoniere
Cochti haer goet ende diere;
Huven, vingherline van goude
Ende chierheit menechfoude.
Om al die chierheit dede hi proeven,
Die eneger bruut soude behoeven.
Met hem nam hi .vc. pont
Ende voer in ere avonstont
Heymelike buten der stede.
Al dat scoonheide voerdi mede
Wel ghetorst op sijn paert
Ende voer alsoo ten cloostere waert,
Daer si seide, inden vergier,
Onder enen eglent
Hi ghinc sitten neder int cruut,
Tote zijn lief soude comen uut.
Van hem latic nu die tale
Ende segghe u vander scoonder smale.
Vore middernacht lude si mettine;
Die minne dede haer grote pine.
Als mettenen waren ghesongen
Beide van ouden ende van iongen
Die daer waren int covent,
Ende si weder waren ghewent
Opten dormter al ghemene,

but he went each day into the town, and he bought blue and scarlet cloth, from which he had a cloak made with a hood, a gown and a jacket, and he had them well lined. No one ever saw finer furs among well-dressed women, and everyone who saw the clothes admired them. He bought for her at great expense a girdle, with scissors and a purse, caps, gold rings and many kinds of ornaments, and he provided all the finery which any bride could need. He took with him five hundred pounds, and one night secretly left the town, carrying all the finery with him, well packed on his horse, and he rode out to the convent, and there where she had said, in the orchard under an eglantine, he sat down on the grass, waiting for his love to come out. Now let me leave him, and continue my story about the lovely young woman. At midnight she rang for matins. Love gave her great sorrow, and when matins had been sung by both the old nuns and the young who were then in the convent, and they had all gone back together to the dormitory,

Bleef si inden co*o*r allene
Ende si sprac haer ghebede,
Alsi te voren dicke dede.
Si knielde vo*o*rden outaer
Ende sprac met groten vaer:
'Maria, moeder, soete name,
Nu en mach minen lichame
Niet langher in dabijt gheduren.
Ghi kint wel in allen uren
Smenschen herte ende sijn wesen;
Ic hebbe ghevast ende ghelesen
Ende ghenomen discipline,
Hets al om niet dat ic pine;
Minne worpt mi onder voet,
Dat ic der werelt dienen moet.
Also*o* waerlike als ghi, here lieve,
Wort ghehanghen tusschen .ij. dieve
Ende aent cruce wort gherecket,
Ende ghi Lazaruse verwecket,
Daer hi lach inden grave do*o*t,
Soe moetti kinnen minen no*o*t
Ende mine mesdaet mi vergheven;
Ic moet in swaren sonden sneven.'
Na desen ghinc si uten core
Teenen beelde, daer si vore
Knielde ende sprac hare ghebede,
Daer Maria stont ter stede.
Si riep: 'Maria!' onversaghet,
'Ic hebbe u nach ende dach geclaghet
Ontfermelike mijn vernoy
Ende mi en es niet te bat een hoy.
Ic werde mijns sins te male quijt,
Blivic langher in dit abijt!'
Die covel to*o*ch si ute al daer

she remained alone in the choir, saying her prayers as she had often done before. She knelt in front of the altar, and said with great anguish: 'Mary, mother, sweet name, my body can no longer endure in this habit. You know well at all times what is in man's heart and what his life is. I have fasted and prayed and scourged myself, but I have tormented myself for nothing; love has conquered me, and I must serve the world. As truly as You, my dear Lord, were stretched and hanged upon the cross between two thieves, as truly as You called Lazarus when he lay dead in his grave, so may You know my need and forgive me my trespass, for I must fall into mortal sin.' And with this she went out of the choir to where the image of Mary stood, and she knelt before it and prayed. Without fear she called out: 'Mary, I have lamented day and night to you, asking for pity in my distress, and I am not a scrap better off for it. I shall go altogether out of my mind if I stay any longer in this habit.' Then she took off all her habit

Ende leidse op onser vrouwen outaer.
Doen dede si ute hare scoen.
Nu hoort, watsi sal doen!
Die slotele vander sacristiën
Hinc si voor dat beelde Mariën;
Ende ic segt u over waar,
Waer omme dat sise hinc al daer:
Ofmense te priemtide sochte,
Dat mense best daer vinden mochte.
Hets wel recht in alder tijt,
Wie vore Mariën beelde lijt,
Dat hi sijn oghen derwaert sla
Ende segge 'ave', eer hi ga,
'Ave Maria': daer omme si ghedinct,
Waer omme dat si die slotel daer hinc.

Nu ghinc si danen dorden noot
Met enen pels al bloot,
Daer si een dore wiste,
Die si ontsloot met liste,
Ende ghincker heymelijc uut,
Stillekine sonder gheluut.
Inden vergier quam si met vare.
Di iongelinc wart haers gheware;
Hi seide: 'lief, en verveert u niet,
Hets u vrient dat ghi hier siet.'
Doen si beide te samen quamen,
Si begonste hare te scamen,
Om dat si in enen pels stoet,
Bloots hooft ende barvoet.
Doen seidi: 'wel scone lichame,
U soo waren bat bequame
Scone ghewaden ende goede cleder.
Hebter mi om niet te leder,

and laid it upon our Lady's altar, and she took off her shoes. Now listen to what she did next: her sacristan's key she hung in front of Mary's image, and I will tell you why she hung it there. It was so that it would most easily be found when they looked for her at prime, for it is an ancient custom that whoever passes in front of Mary's image should lift up his eyes to it and say an Ave, Maria before he goes, and that was why she thought of hanging the key there.

Then there was nothing else for her but to go, dressed only in her shift, to where she knew there was a door which she had the trick of opening, and so she stole out without making a sound and came timidly into the orchard. The young man saw her, and said: 'Dear, do not be frightened; it is me, your love, whom you can see.' As they met, she was filled with shame to be standing there in her shift, bareheaded and barefooted; and then he said, 'Your lovely body deserves fine dresses and good clothing; and do not be angry with me on this account,

Ic salse u gheven sciere.'
Doe ghinghen si onder den eglentiere
Ende alles, dies si behoeft,
Des gaf hi hare ghenoech.
Hi gaf haer cleder twee paer,
Blau waest dat si aen dede daer,
Wel ghescepen int ghevoech.
Vriendelike hi op haer loech.
Hi seide: 'lief, dit hemelblau
Staet u bat dan dede dat grau.'
Twee cousen tooch si ane
Ende twee scoen cordewane
Die hare vele bat stonden
Dna scoen die waren ghebonden.
Hoot cleder van witter ziden
Gaf hi hare te dien tiden,
Die si op haer hooft hinc.
Doen cussese die ionghelinc
Vriendelike aen haren mont.
Hem dochte, daer si voor hem stont,
Dat die dach verclaerde.
Haestelike ghinc hi tsinen paerde,
Hi settese voor hem int ghereide.
Dus voren si henen beide,
Soe verre, dat began te daghen,
Dat si hen nyemen volghen en saghen.
Doen begant te lichtene int oost.
Si seide: 'God, alder werelt troos,
Nu moeti ons bewaren,
Ic sie den dach verclaren.
Waric met u nietcomen uut,
Ic soude prime hebben gheluut,
Als ic wilen was ghewone
Inden clooster van religione.

for I shall give you beautiful thing.' So they went under the eglantine, and everything which she needed, he gave her in great plenty. He gave her two gowns, and it was the blue one which she put on then, well and fittingly made. He looked lovingly at her and said, 'Dear, sky-blue suits you better than grey.' She put on a pair of stockings, and a pair of fine shoes, which suited her better than her sandals. Then he gave her veils of white silk, with which she covered her head. Then the young man lovingly kissed her lips, and it seemed to him as she stood there before him that the day was breaking. Quickly he went to his horse, and set her in front of him in the saddle, and so they both rode so far that as it began to dawn they saw that no one was following them. When the east began to grow light, she said: 'God, comfort of the whole world, guard us now. I see the day dawning, and had I not run away with you, I should have rung the bell for prime as I used to in our convent.

I think that I shall repent this journey, for there is little faith in the world, to which I have now confided myself: it is like those dishonest traders who sell rings made of base metal for gold.'

Ic ducht mi die vaert sal rouwen:
Die werelt hout soo cleine trouwe,
Al hebbic mi ghekeert daeran;
Si slacht den losen coman,
Die vingherline van formine
Vercoopt voor guldine.'

'Ay, wat segdi, suverlike,
Ocht ic u emmermeer beswike,
Soo moete mi God scinden!
Waer dat wi ons bewinden,
In scede van u te ghere noot,
Ons en scede die bitter doot!
Hoe mach u aen mi twien?
Ghi en hebt aen mi niet versien,
Dat ic u fel was ofte loos.
Sint dat ic u ierst vercoos,
En haddic niet in minen sinne
Ghedaen een keyserinne.
Op dat ic haers werdech ware,
Lief, en liete u niet om hare!
Des moghedi seker wesen.
Ik vore met ons ute ghelesen
.Vc. pont wit selverijn,
Daer seldi, lief, vrouwe af sijn.
Al varen wie in vremde lande,
Wine derven verteren ghene pande
Binnen desen seven iaren.'
Dus quamen si den telt ghevaren
Smorgens aen een foreest,
Daer die voghele hadden feest.
Si maecten soo groot ghescal,
Datment hoorde over al.
Elc sanc na der naturen sine.

'Ah, what are you saying, my lovely one? If ever I were to betray you, so may God destroy me! Wherever we may go, I shall not leave you under any circumstances, unless cruel death part us. How can you doubt me? You have never found me cruel or false to you, and since I first chose you, I would not have set my mind upon an empress, had I been worthy of her, nor would I have left you for her, my dear one. Of this you may be sure. I have taken care to bring with us five hundred pounds in pure silver, and of this you shall be the mistress, dear one. Even though we travel abroad, we shall not need to sell anything for the next seven years.'

So, as they galloped on, they came during the morning to a forest in which the birds were rejoicing. They made such a tumult that one could hear it everywhere, as each one sang according to its kind.

Daer stonden scone bloemkine
Op dat groene velt ontploken,
Die scone waren ende suete roken.
Die locht was claer ende scone.
Daer stonden vele rechte bome,
Die ghelovert waren rike.
Die ionghelinc sach op die suverlike,
Daer hi ghestade minne toe droech.
Hi seide: 'lief, waert u ghevoech,
Wi souden beeten ende bloemen lesen,
Het dunct mi hier scone wesen.
Laet ons spelen der minnen spel.'
'Wat segdi', sprac si, 'dorper fel,
Soudic beeten op tfelt,
Ghelijc enen wive die wint ghelt
Dorperlijc met haren lichame,
Seker, soo haddic cleine scame!
Dit en ware u niet ghesciet,
Waerdi van dorpers aerde niet!
Ic mach mi bedinken onsochte.
Godsat hebdi diet sochte!
Swighet meer deser talen
Ende hoort die voghele inden dalen,
Hoe si singhen ende hem vervroyen.
Die tijt sal u te min vernoyen,
Alsic bi u ben al naect
Op een bedde wel ghemaect,
Soo doet al dat u ghenoecht
Ende dat uwer herten voeght.
Ic hebs in mijn herte toren,
Dat ghijt mi heden leit te voren.'

Hi seide: 'lief en belghet u niet.
Het dede Venus, diet mi riet.

Lovely flowers stood everywhere, blossoming upon the green field, beautiful to see and sweet to smell. The air was clear and bright, and many tall trees, richly leaved, stood there. The young man looked upon the beautiful young woman for whom he felt a constant love, and he said: 'Beloved, if it would please you to dismount and gather some flowers, this seems to me to be a good place; and here let us play the game of love.' She said, 'Why are you talking like a crude village lout? Do you expect me to dismount here, in the fields, like a peasant woman who earns money with her body? Indeed, I should have little modesty to do that. Such a thing would never have occurred to you if you were not yourself a peasant by nature. I may well repent what I have done. God's curse on you who wished for such a thing. Speak no more of such matters, and listen to how the birds in this valley sing and rejoice, and so the time will pass pleasantly for you. When I lie naked beside you in a well-made bed, then do everything that you please and which your heart longs for. But it is a grief in my heart that you have suggested this to me.'

He said: 'Beloved, do not be angry. It was Venus who prompted me to this.

God geve mi scande ende plaghe,
Ochtic[s] u emmermeer ghewaghe.'
Si seide: 'ic vergheeft u dan,
Ghi sijt mijn troost voor alle man
Die leven onder den trone.
Al levede Absolon die scone
Ende ic des wel seker ware
Met hem te levene .M. iare
In weelden ende in rusten,
Ic liets mi niet ghecusten.
Lief, ic hebbe u soo vercoren,
Men mocht mi dat niet legghen voren,
Dat ic uwes soude vergheten.
Waric in hemelrike gheseten
Ende ghi hier in ertrike,
Ic quame tot u sekerlike!
Ay God, latet onghewroken
Dat ic dullijc hebbe ghesproken!
Die minste bliscap in hemelrike
En es hier ghere vrouden ghelike;
Daer es die minste soo volmaect,
Datter zielen niet en smaect
Dan Gode te minnen sonder inde.
Al erdsche dinc es ellinde,
Si en dooghet niet een haer
Jeghen die minste die es daer.
Diere om pinen die sijn vroet,
Al eest dat ic dolen moet
Ende mi te groten sonden keren
Dore u, lieve scone ionchere.'

Dus hadden si tale ende wedertale.
Si reden berch ende dale.
In can u niet ghesegghen wel

May God send me dreadful punishment if ever I dare to do such a thing again.' She said: 'Then I forgive you, for you are my comfort, above every man living under heaven. Even if the beautiful Absolom were alive, and I were sure of living with him for a thousand years, that would not compensate me for you. My dear one, I have loved you so dearly that no one could persuade me that I might ever forget you. Even if I were established in heaven, if you were here upon earth I should come to you without fail. Oh God, do not punish me for the folly I have spoken: there is no joy here to compare with the least of heaven's joys. The least joy there is so perfect that the soul asks for nothing than to love God everlastingly. Every earthly joy is exile, and not worth a straw compared with heaven's least joy, and those who long for such joys are wise. Yet I am forced to go astray and to choose a life of great sin for love of you, dear and lovely lord.'

So they rode over mountains and through valleys, conversing with one another, and I cannot well tell you

Wat tusschen hen tween ghevel.
Si voren alsoo voort,
Tes si quamen in een poort,
Die scone stont in enen dale.
Daer soo bequaemt hem wale,
Dat siere bleven der iaren seven
Ende waren in verweenden leven
Met ghenuechten van lichamen,
Ende wonnen .ij. kinder tsamen.
Daer, na den seven iaren,
Alse die penninghen verteert waren,
Moesten si teren vanden pande,
Die si brachten uten lande.
Cleder, scoonheit ende paerde
Vercochten si te halver warde
Ende brochtent al over saen.
Doen en wisten si wat bestaen;
Si en conste ghenen roc spinenn,
Daer si met mochte winnen.
Die tijt wart inden lande diere
Van spisen, van wine ende ban viere
Ende van al datmen eten mochte.
Dies hem wart te moede onsochte;
Si waren hem liever vele doot,
Dan si hadden ghebeden broot.
Die aermoede maecte een ghesceet
Tusschen hem beiden, al waest hem leet.
Aenden man ghebrac dierste trouwe;
Hi lietse daer in groten rouwe
Ende voer te sinen lande weder.
Si en sachen met oghen nye zeder.
Daer bleven met hare ghinder
Twee uter maten scone kinder.

all that was said between them. They travelled on until they came to a town, finely situated in a valley, which pleased them so well that they lived there for seven years, living a life of pleasure and bodily delights, and they had two children. But after seven years, when all their money was spent, they had to live by pledging what they had brought with them. Clothing, jewels and horses they sold for half their value, and soon they had used up that money. They did not know what to do. She could not spin and earn money that way. At that time prices were high in the region: food, wine, beer, everything needed for sustenance was dear. This was a great distress to them, for they would rather have died than have begged for bread. Poverty made division between them, much though it hurt them. It was the man who first broke faith. He left her there in great misery and returned to his own country. She never saw him again; and she remained behind there with her two children, who were very beautiful.

Si sprac: 'hets mi comen toe,
Dat ic duchte spade ende vroe;
Ic ben in vele doghens bleven.
Die ghene heeft mi begheven,
Daer ic mi trouwen to verliet.
Maria, vrouwe, oft ghi ghebiet,
Bidt vore mi ende mine .ij. ionghere.
Dat wi niet en sterven van hongere.
Wat salic doen, elendech wijf!
Ic moet beide, ziele ende lijf,
Bevlecken met sondeghen daden.
Maria, vrouwe, staet mi in staden!
Al constic enen roc spinnen,
In mochter niet met winnen
In tween weken een broot.
Ic moet gaen dorden noot
Buten der stat op tfelt
Ende winnen met minen lichame ghelt,
Daer ic met mach copen spise.
In mach in ghere wise
Mijn kinder niet begheven.'
Dus ghinc si in een sondech leven.
Want men seit ons overwaer,
Dat si langhe seve iaer
Ghemene wijf ter werelt ghinc
 Ende meneghe sonde ontfinc,
Dat haer was wel onbequame,
Die si dede metten lichame,
Daer si cleine ghenuechte hadde in;
Al dede sijt om een cranc ghewin,
Daersi haer kinder met onthelt.
Wat holpt al vertelt
Die scamelike sonden ende die zwaer,
Daer si in was .XIIIJ. iaer!

Then she said: 'Now what I feared, late and early, has come upon me. Here I am in great suffering, and he whom I put my trust in has deserted me. Mary, Lady, if it be your will, pray for me and my two children, that we do not die of hunger. What should I do, miserable woman? I have made my immortal soul and my days on earth foul with my sinful deeds. Mary, Lady, be my help! Even if I did know how to spin, I could not earn enough in two weeks to buy one loaf. Necessity forces me to go out of the town to the fields, and sell my body for money so that I can buy food. Under no circumstances can I abandon my children.' So she embarked upon a sinful life, and they tell us that for the next seven years she lived as a common whore, and committed many sins. What she did with her body was a misery to her in which she took no pleasure. She only did it so as to scrape a bare living and to keep her children. What would be the profit of enumerating the great and horrible sins in which she lived for fourteen years?

Maer emmer en lietsi achter niet,
Hadsi rouwe oft verdriet,
Sine las alle daghe met trouwen
Die seven ghetiden van onser vrouwen.
Die las si haer te loven ende teren,
Dat sise moeste bekeren
Uten sondeliken daden,
Daer si was met beladen
Bi ghetale .XIIIJ. iar;
Dat segghic u over waer.
Si was seven iaer metten man,
Die .ij. kindere an hare wan,
Diese liet in ellinde,
Daer si doghede groot meswinde.
Dierste .VIJ. iaer hebdi gehoort;
Verstaet hoe si levede voort.

Als die ·XIIIJ. iaer waren gedaen,
Sinde haer God int herte saen
Berouwennesse alsoo groot,
Dat si met euen swerde al bloot
Liever liete haer hoot af slaən,
Dan si meer sonden hadde ghecaen
Met haren lichame, alsi plach
Si weende nacht eede dach,
Dat haer oghen selden drogheded.
Si seids: 'Maria, die Gode soghede,
Fonteyne boven alle wiven,
Laet mi inder noot niet bliven!
Vrouwe ,ic neme u torconden,
Dat mi rouwen mine sonden
Ende sijn mi herde leet.
Der es soo vele, dat ic en weet
Waer icse dede ocht met wien.

But always, however great her miseries might be, she never forgot to read each day with devotion the seven hours of our Lady, which she read to Mary's praise and honour, asking her to turn her away from the sinful deeds with which she had been oppressed for a full fourteen years. What I have told you is true: she lived seven years with the man who begot two children by her, and who left her in destitution through which she suffered great distress. You have been told of the first seven years, and you know how she lived after that.

When the fourteen years were over, God suddenly sent into her heart such great contrition that she would rather have suffered her head to bec ut off with a naked sword than go on committing carnal sins as she had done. She wept night and day, so that her eyes were seldom dry. She said: 'Mary, who suckled God, you pure spring, beyond all women, let me not remain in need! Lady, I call you to witness my contrition for my sins and the sorrows of my heart. My sins are so many that I do not know where I committed them or with whom.

Ay lacen! wat sal mijns ghescien!
Ic mach wel ieghen dordeel sorgen —
Doghen Gods zijn mi verborgen —,
Daer sonden selen bliken,
Beide van armen ende van riken,
Ende alle mesdaet sal sijn ghewroken,
Daer en si vore biechte af ghesproken
Ende penitencie ghedaen.
Dat wetic wel, sonder waen.
Des benic in groten vare.
Al droghic alle daghe een hare,
Ende crooper met van lande te lande
Over voete ende over hande
Wullen, barvoet, sonder scoen,
Nochtan en constic niet ghedoen,
Dat ic van sonden worde vri,
Maria, vrouwe, ghi en troost mi,
Fonteyne boven alle doghet!
Ghi hebt den meneghen verhoghet,
Alse wel Teophuluse sceen;
Hi was der quaetster sonderen een
Ende haddem den duvel op ghegeven,
Beide ziele ende leven,
Ende was worden sijn man;
  Vrouwe, ghi verloosseten nochtan.
Al benic een besondech wijf
Ende een onghetroost keytijf,
In wat leven ic noy[t] was,
Vrouwe, ghedinct dat ic las
Tuwer eren een ghebede!
Toont aen mi u ootmoedechede!
Ic ben ene die es bedroevet
Ende uwer hulpen wel behoevet;
Dies maghic mi verbouden:

Alas, what is to become of me! I may well dread that Day of Judgment, for God's mercy is hidden from me, and all sins will then be shown, both of the poor and of the rich, and every misdeed will be avenged unless it has before been revealed at confession, and penance performed. I know very well that this is true, and I am in great fear on account of it. Though I were to wear a hair shirt every day, though I were to go crawling from country to country on my hands and knees, clad in coarse clothes and barefooted, still I could not do enough to free myself from my sins. Mary, Lady, be my consolation, you pure spring, beyond all virtue! You have brought gladness to many, as appeared indeed through Theophilus, who was one of the worst of sinners, and had surrendered himself soul and body to the devil and had become his servant; yet, Lady, you did not abandon him. Though I am a sinful woman and an abandoned wretch, whatever kind of life I lived, still remember, Lady, that I used to say a prayer in honour of you. Look on me in clemency. I am an afflicted one, in great need of your help. I may make bold to ask this:

En bleef hem nye onvergouden,
Die u gruete, maget vrië,
Alle daghe met ere ave marië.
Die u ghebet gherne lesen,
Sie mooghen wel seker wesen,
Dat hem daer af sal comen vrame.
Vrouwe, hets u soo wel bequame,
Uut vercorne Gods bruut.
U sone sinde u een saluut
Te Nazaret, daer hi u sochte,
Die u ene bootscap brochte,
Die nye van bode was ghehoort;
Daer omme sijn u die selve woort
Soo bequame sonder wanc,
Dat ghijs wet elken danc,
Die u gheerne daer mede quet.
Al waer hi in sonden belet,
Ghi souten te ghenaden bringhen
Ende voor uwen sone verdinghen.'
Dese bedinghe ende dese claghe
Dreef die sondersse alle daghe.
Si nam een kint in elke hant,
Ende ghincker met door tlant,
In armoede, van stede te steden,
Ende levede bider beden.
Soo langhe dolede si achter dlant,
Dat si den clooster weder vant,
Daer si hadde gheweest nonne,
Ende quam daer savons na der sonne
In ere weduwen huus spade,
Daer si bat herberghe door ghenade,
Dat si daer snachts mochte bliven.
'Ic mocht u qualijc verdriven,'
Sprac die weduwe, 'met uwen kinderkinen.

do not leave them unrewarded, the greetings I gave to you every day with an Ave, Maria. Those who say your prayer with devotion may be very sure that help will come to them from this. Lady, chosen bride of God, this is very pleasing to you. Your Son sent you a greeting to Nazareth, where He sought you, and brought you such a message as was never before heard of any messenger. Therefore the very words of that message are beyond doubt so pleasing to you that you are full of every gratitude to those who greet you with them. However bogged down in sin, you would bring them into grace and intercede for them before your Son.' Daily this sinful woman offered up these petitions and lamentations.

She took a child in either hand, and with them she wandered through the country, in poverty, going from place to place and living by begging; and she wandered around the country until she came back to the monastery where she had been a nun; and late one evening, after sunset, she came to the house of a widow whom she asked for shelter out of kindness, if she might stay there the night. 'I could hardly send you away with your little children,' the widow said.

Mi dunct dat si moede scinen.
Ruust u ende sit neder.
Ic sal u deilen weder
Dat mi verleent onse here
Door siere liever moeder ere.'
Dus bleef si met haren kinden
Ende soude gheerne ondervinden,
Hoet inden clooster stoede.
'Segt mi,' seitsi, 'vrouwe goede,
Es dit covint van ioffrouwen?'
'Jaet,' seitsi, 'bi miere trouwen.
Dat verweent es ende rike;
Men weet niewer sijns ghelike.
Die nonnen diere abijt in draghen,
In hoorde nye ghewaghen
Van hen gheen gherochten
Dies si blame hebben mochten.'

Die daer bi haren kinderen sat,
Si seide: 'waer bi segdi dat?
Ic hoorde binnen deser weken
Soo vele van ere nonnen spreken;
Alsic verstoet in minen sinne,
Soo was si hier costerinne.
Diet mi seide hine looch niet:
Hets binnen .XIIIJ. iaren ghesciet,
Dat si uten clooster streec.
Men wiste noyt, waer si weec
Oft in wat lande si inde nam.'
Doen wert die weduwe gram
Ende seide: 'ghi dunct mi reven!
Derre talen seldi begheven
Te segghene vander costerinnen
Oft ghi en blijft hier niet binnen!

'You seem to me to be tired. Sit down and rest. I will give you a share of what I have, and our Lord will repay me to the honour of His dear mother.' So she stayed there with her children, and she dearly wanted to find out how things were in the monastery. 'Tell me,' she said, 'good woman, is this a convent of virgins?' 'Yes,' she replied, 'it is indeed, and a rich and splendid one. No one ever saw its like; and no one ever heard anyone dare to speak ill of the nuns who live there, so as to bring them into disrepute.'

The woman sitting there with her children said: 'How can you say that? Only this week I heard such things said about a nun that I was astounded, and she was sacristan here. The person who told me was not lying. It is now fourteen years ago since she ran away from the monastery, and nobody knew where she fled to or in what country she ended.' Then the widow became angry, and said: 'I think you must be mad! Either you stop telling such stories about the sacristan, or you do not remain in this house!

Si heeft hier costersse ghesijn
.XIIIJ. iaer den termijn,
Dat men haers noyt ghemessen conde
In alden tiden éne metten stonde,
Hen si dat si waer onghesont.
Hi ware erger dan een hont,
Diere af seide el dan goet;
Si draghet soo reynen moet,
Die eneghe nonne draghen mochte.
Die alle die cloosters dore sochte,
Die staen tusschen Elve ende der Geronde
Ic wane men niet vinden en conde
Neghene die gheesteliker leeft!'

Die alsoo langhe hadde ghesneeft
Dese tale dochte haer wesen wonder,
Ende seide: 'vrouwe, maect mi conder.
Hoe hiet haer moeder ende vader?'
Doe noemesise beide gader.
Doen wiste si wel, dat si haer meende.
Ay God! hoe si snachs weende
Heymelike voor haer bedde!
Si seide: 'ic en habbe ander wedde
Dan van herten groot berouwe.
Sijt in mijn hulpe, Maria, vrouwe!
Mijn sonden sijn mi soo leet,
Saghic enen hoven heet,
Die in groten gloyen stonde,
Dat die vlamme ghinghe uten monde,
Ic croper in met vlite,
Mochtic mier sonden werden quite.
Here, ghi hebt wanhope verwaten,
Daer op willic mi verlaten!
Ic ben, die altoos ghenade hoopt,

She has been sacristan now these fourteen years, and in all that time sickness has never made her absent from her duties for as long as one mass. Anyone who said anything other than good of her would be madder than a dog. Her disposition is as pure as that of any nun. If you were to search in all the nunneries between the Elbe and the Gironde, I do not believe that you could find anyone living a more spiritual life!'

This story amazed the woman, who had for so long lived in sin, and she said: 'Good woman, assure me about this. What were the names of her father and mother?' Then the other named them both, and she knew well that it was she herself who was meant. Oh God, how she wept that night in secret beside her bed! She said: 'My only possession is great contrition of heart. Mary, Lady, come to my help! My sins are so hateful to me that if I were to see a fiery furnace standing glowing with flames belching out, I would gladly crawl inside it if I could so be free of my sins. Lord, You have forbidden us to despair, and in that will I put my trust. Always I hope for Your grace,

Al eest dat mi anxt noopt
Ende mi bringt in groten vare.
En was nye soo groten sondare,
Sint dat ghi op ertrike quaemt
Ende menschelike vorme naemt
Ende ghi aen den cruce wout sterven,
Sone lieti den sondare niet bederven;
Die met berouwenesse socht gnade,
Hi vantse, al quam hi spade,
Alst wel openbaer scheen
Den enen sondare vanden tween,
 Die tuwer rechter siden hinc.
Dats ons een troostelijc dinc,
Dat ghine ontfinc[t] onbescouden.
Goet berou mach als ghewouden;
Dat maghic merken an desen.
Ghi seit: 'vrient, du salt wesen
Met mi heden in mijn rike,
Dat segghic u ghewaerlike.'
Noch, here, waest openbare,
Dat Gisemast, die mordenare,
Ten lesten om ghenade bat.
Hi gaf u weder gout no scat,
Dan hem berouden sine sonden.
U ontfermecheit en es niet te gronden
Niet meer, dan men mach
Die zee uut sceppen op enen dach
Ende droghen al toten gronde.
Dus was nye soo grote sonde,
Vrouwe, u ghenaden en gaen boven.
Hoe soudic dan sijn verscoven
Van uwer ontfermecheit,
Ocht mi mijn sonden sijn soo leit!'

even though I am dogged by fear and brought into great terror. There was never any sinner so great that You would abandon him to perdition, since You came upon earth and took human form and were willing to die upon the Cross. If such a sinner with repentance sought grace, he found it, however late he might seek for it, as it plainly was shown by that one of the two malefactors who hung at Your right hand. It is for us great consolation that You received him and forgave him. Perfect contrition is of great power, as I can see from this. You said: 'Friend, truly I say to you that you will be with Me today in My kingdom.' And it was plain, Lord, that Dismas, this murderer, asked for Your grace in the end. He offered You neither gold nor silver, only his repentance for his sins. We can no more measure Your mercy than we can in a single day shift and dry up the deep sea. Nor was there ever, Lady, sin so great that it exceeded your pity. How then should I be thrust out from your clemency, if my sins are so hateful to me?'

Daer si lach in dit ghebede,
Quam een vaec in al haer lede
Ende si wart in lape sochte.
In enen vysioen haer dochte,
Hoe een stemme aan haer riep,
Daer si lach ende sliep:
'Mensche, du heves soo langhe gecarmt,
Dat Maria dijns ontfarmt,
Want si heeft u verbeden.
Gaet inden clooster met haestecheden:
Ghi vint die doren open wide,
Daer ghi uut ginges ten selven tide
Met uwen lieve, den ionghelinc,
Die u inder noot af ghinc.
Al dijn abijt vinstu weder
Ligghen opten outaer neder;
Wile, covele ende scoen
Mooghedi coenlijc ane doen;
Des danct hooghelike Mariën:
Die slotele vander sacristiën,
Die ghi voor tbeelde hinct
Snachs, doen ghi uut ghinct,
Die heeft si soo doen bewaren,
Datmen binnen .XIIIJ. iaren
Uwes nye en ghemiste,
Soo dat yemen daer af wiste.
Maria es soo wel u vrient:
Si heeft altoos voor u ghedient
Min no meer na dijn ghelike.
Dat heeft de vrouwe van hemelrike,
Sonderse, door u ghedaen!
Si heet u inden clooster gaen.
Ghi en vint nyeman op u bedde.
Hets van Gode, dat ic u quedde!'

So she lay prostrate at her prayers, until slumber overcame her whole body and she slept peacefully; and then it seemed to her as if in a vision a voice called to her as she lay asleep: 'Woman, you have entreated for so long that Mary has had pity on you and interceded for you. Go at once to the monastery, and you will find the doors wide open at the same hour as you ran away with the young man your paramour, when you went off to a life of misery. You will find all your habit still laid out on the altar, your veil and cowl and shoes; have no fear but put them on, and say fervent thanks to Mary for this. And she has so taken care of the sacristan's key which you hung before her image on that night when you ran away that no one has missed you in fourteen years or knew what happened to you. Mary is such a friend to you that all this time she has done your office for you, just as you did it, neither less nor more. This is what the mistress of Heaven has done for you, a sinner! Now she orders you to go back to the monastery, where you will find no one sleeping in your bed. What I have told you is a message from God.'

Na desen en waest niet lanc,
Dat si uut haren slape ontspranc.
Si seide: 'God, gheweldechere,
En ghehinct den duvel nemmermere,
Dat hi mi bringhe in mere verdriet,
Dan mi nu es ghesciet!
Ochtic nu inden clooster ghinghe
Ende men mi over dieveghe vinghe,
Soo waric noch meer ghescent,
Dan doen ic ierst rumde covent.
Ic mane u, God die goede,
Dor uwen pretiosen bloede,
Dat uut uwer ziden liep,
Ocht die stemme, die aen mi riep,
Hier es comen te minen baten,
Dat sijs niet en moete laten,
Si en come anderwerf tot hare
Ende derde werven openbare,
Soo dat ic mach sonder waen
Weder in minen clooster gaen.
Ic wilre om benediën
Ende loven altoos Mariën!'

Sanders snachts, moghedi horen,
Quam haer een stemme te voren,
Die op haer riep ende seide:
'Mensche, du maecs te langhe beide!
Ganc weder in dinen clooster,
God sal wesen dijn trooster.
Doet dat Maria u ontbiet!
Ic ben haer bode, en twivels niet.'
Nu heefsise anderwerf vernomen
Die stemme tote haer comen
Ende hietse inden clooster gaen;

Soon after this she started up out of her sleep, and said: 'God, almighty ruler, do not permit the devil to bring me into greater misery than I am in now. If I were to go back to the monastery now and they were to apprehend me as a thief, I should be in a worse state than when first I fled from the convent. I entreat you, my good God, by the Precious Blood which flowed from Your side, if the voice which called to me has come to me to help me, that You do not suffer it to be silent, but let it speak a second and a third time, clearly, so that I may go back to my monastery without fear; and in return I shall always bless and praise Mary.'

On the next night, you may hear, a voice sounded to her, calling for her and saying: 'Woman, you are delaying too long! Go back to your monastery, and God will comfort you. Do as Mary commands you. I am her messenger; you need not doubt.' So she understood once again the voice which spoke to her and commanded her to go into the monastery;

Nochtan en dorst sijs niet bestaen.
Der derder nacht verbeyt si noch
Ende seide: 'eest elfs ghedroch,
Dat mi comt te voren,
Soo maghic cortelike scoren
Des duvels ghewelt ende sine cracht
Ende ocht hire comt te nacht,
Here, soo maecten soo confuus,
Dat hi vare uten huus,
Dat hi mi niet en moete scaden.
Maria, nu staet mi in staden,
Die ene stemme ane mi sint,
Ende hiet mi gaen int covint;
Ic mane u, vrouwe, bi uwen kinde,
Dat ghise mi derdewerven wilt sinden.'

Doen waecte si den derden nacht.
Een stemme quam van gods cracht
Met enen over groten lichte
Ende seide: 'hets bi onrechte,
Dat ghi niet en doet dat ic u hiet,
Want u Maria bi mi ontbiet.
Ghi moocht beiden te lanc.
Gaet inden clooster, sonder wanc,
Ghi vint die doren op ende wide ontdaen,
Daer ghi wilt, moghedi gaen.
U abijt vindi weder
Ligghende opten outaer neder.'
Als die stemme dit hadde gheseit,
Mochte die zondersse die daer leit,
Die claerheit metten oghen wel sien;
Si seide: 'nu en darf mi niet twien,
Dese stemme comt van Gode,
Ende es der maghet Mariën bode.

but still she did not dare to do it. She waited for the third night, and said: 'If it is the deceit of some evil spirit which manifests itself to me, then let me soon overcome the devil's power and cunning, and if he should appear again tonight, Lord, vanquish him so that he flee from the house, so that he cannot harm me. Mary, come to my help now: you who sent a voice to me, bidding me go to the monastery, I entreat you, Lady, by your Child that you send the voice to me a third time.'

Then on the third night she kept watch, and through the power of God a voice came, with a dazzling light, and said: 'For shame that you have not done as I commanded you, as Mary bade you through me. You may delay too long. Go back to the monastery without fear, and you will find the doors opened wide, so that you can go wherever you choose. You will find your habit still laid out on the altar.' When the voice had said this, the sinful woman, lying there, could clearly see the light; and she said: 'I no longer dare doubt that this voice comes from God and is the messenger of the Virgin Mary.

Dat wetic nu sonder hone.
Si comt met lichte soo scone:
Nu en willics niet laten,
Ic wille mi inden clooster maken,
Ic saelt ooc doen in goeder trouwen
Opten troost van onser vrouwen,
Ende wille mijn kinder beide gader
Bevelen Gode onsen Vader.
Hi salse wel bewaren.'
Doen tooch si ute al sonder sparen
Haer cleder, daer sise met decte
Heymelike, dat sise niet en wecte.
Si cussese beide aen haren mont.
Si seide: 'kinder, blijft ghesont.
Op den troost van onser vrouwen
Latic u hier in goeder trouwen,
En hadde mi Maria niet verbeden,
Ic en hadde u niet begheven
Om al tgoet, dat Rome heeft binnen.'
Hoort, wes si sal beghinnen.

Nu gaet si met groten weene
Ten clooster waert, moeder eene.
Doen si quam inden vergiere,
Vant si die dore ontsloten sciere.
Si ghincker in sonder wanc:
'Maria, hebbes danc,
Ic ben comen binnen mure;
God gheve mi goede aventure!'
Waer si quam, vant si die dore
Al wide open ieghen hore.
In die kerke si doe trac;
Heymelike si doe sprac:
'God here, ic bidde u met vlite,

Now I know that without any fear of deceit, because it comes accompanied by this lovely light. Now I shall no longer delay, but make my way to the monastery; and I shall do this in good faith, trusting to our Lady, and I shall commend my two children to God our Father, and He will take good care of them.' Then she took off all her clothing, and quietly covered her children with it, so that they did not wake. She kissed them both on the lips, and she said: 'Children, farewell. I leave you here in good faith, trusting in our Lady. Had Mary not ordered me to do this, I would not have forsaken you for all the wealth in Rome.' Listen to what happened to her next.

This mother bereft of her children makes her way to the monastery weeping greatly, and when she entered the orchard she found the door wide open. She entered without fear, saying: 'Mary, thanks be to you that I am inside the wall. God give me good speed!' As she went on, she found all the doors wide open to greet her, and when she entered the church, she whispered: 'Lord God, I greatly entreat You

Hulpt mi weder im minen abite,
Dat ic over .XIIIJ. iaer
Liet ligghen op onser vrouwen outaer,
Snachs, doen ic danen sciet!'
Dit en es gheloghen niet,
Ic segt u sonder ghile:
Scone, covele ende wile
Vant si ter selver stede weder,
Daer sijt hadde gheleit neder.
Si treact an haestelike
Ende seide: 'God van hemelrike
Ende Maria, maghet fijn,
Ghebenedijt moetti sijn!
Ghi sijt alre doghet bloeme!
In uwen reine magedoeme
Droeghedi een kint sonder wee,
Dat here sal bliven emmermee;
Ghi sijt een uut vercoren werde,
U kint maecte hemel ende erde.
Deze ghewelt comt u van Gode
Ende staet altoos tuwen ghebode.
Den here, die ons broeder
Moghedi ghebieden als moeder
Ende hi u heten lieve dochter.
Hier omme levic vele te sochter.
Wie aen u soect ghenade,
Hi vintse, al comt hi spade.
U hulpe die es alte groot;
Al hebbic vernoy ende noot,
Hets bi u ghewandelt soo,
Dat ic nu mach wesen vroo.
Met rechte maghic u benediën!'
Die slotele vander sacristiën
Sach si hanghen, in ware dine,

to help me to regain my habit, which fourteen years ago I lying on our Lady's altar, on the night when I ran away from here!' What I tell you is no lie or deception: shoes, cowl and veil she found in the very same place as she had once laid them down. Quickly she put them on, and said: 'God of Heaven, and Mary, sweet Virgin, blessed may You be. Mary, flower of every virtue, in your pure virginity you bore a child with no pain, who shall be Lord for evermore; you are a treasure beyond price, for your Child created heaven and earth. This power comes to you from God, and is always ready at your command. That Lord who became our brother you can command as a mother, and He can call you His dear daughter. This is my consolation, for whoever asks compassion from you will find it, however late he comes. Your help is very great indeed, for whatever distress and need I was in, you have so transformed it that now I can rejoice and truly I may bless you.' Her sacristan's key she saw hanging, truly,

Vor Mariën, daer sise hinc.
Die slotele hinc si aen hare
Ende ghinc ten core, daersi clare
Lampten sach berren in allen hoeken.
Daer na ghinc si ten boeken
Ende leide elc op sine stde,
Alsi dicke te voren dede,
Ende si bat der maghet Mariën,
Dat sise van evele moeste vriën
Ende haer kinder, die si liet
Ter weduwen huus in zwaer verdriet.
Binnen dien was die nacht ghegaen,
Dat dorloy begonste te slaen,
Daermen middernacht bi kinde.
Si nam cloczeel biden inde
Ende luude metten so wel te tiden,
Dat sijt hoorden in allen ziden.
Die boven opten dormter laghen,
Die quam[en] alle sonder traghen
Vanden dormter ghemene.
Sine wisten hier af groot no clene.
Si bleef inden clooster haren tijt,
Sonder lachter ende verwijt:
Maria hadde ghedient voor hare,
Ghelijc oft sijt selve ware.
Dus was die sonderse bekeert,
Maria te love, die men eert,
Der maghet van hemelrike,
Die altoos ghetrouwelike
Haren vrient staet in staden,
Alsi in node sijn verladen.

Dese ioffrouwe, daer ic af las,
Es nonne alsi te voren was.

before Mary's image where she had hung it, and she went into the choir, where she saw bright lamps burning in every corner. Then she went for the books and laid each one in its place, as she often had done before, and she prayed the Virgin Mary that she might be made free of all evil, and her children also, whom she had left with a heavy heart at the widow's house. In the meantime, the night had advanced, so that the clock began to strike, to announce to men that it was midnight, and she grasped the end of the bell-rope and rang for office so well that they heard it everywhere, and those who were asleep upstairs in the dormitory all came down together without delay. No one, great or small, knew anything about this. So she was able to live her days in the monastery without scorn or reproof. Mary had served for her, just as if she were Beatrice herself; and in this way was this sinful woman converted, to the glory of Mary, to whom men pay honour, the Virgin of Heaven, who always faithfully comes to the aid of her friends when they are brought into distress.

So this young woman of whom I have been telling you became a nun again as she was before;

Nu en willic vergheten niet
Haer twee kindere, die si liet
Ter weduwen huus in groter noot.
Si en hadden ghelt noch broot.
In can u niet vergronden,
Doen si haer moeder niet en vonden,
Wat groter rouwe datsi dreven.
Die weduwe ghincker sitten neven:
Si hadder op ontfermenisse.
Si seide: 'ic wille toter abdisse
Gaen met desen .ij. kinden.
God sal hare int herte sinden,
Dat si hen goet sal doen.'
Si deden ane cleder ende scoen,
Si ghincker met in covent;
Si seide: 'vrouwe, nu bekent
Den noot van desen tween wesen:
Die moeder heefse met vresen
Te nacht in mijn huus g[h]elaten
Ende es ghegaen hare straten,
Ic en weet, west noch oost.
Dus sijn die kinder onghetroost.
Ic hulpe hen gheerne, wistic hoe.'
De abdisse spracker toe:
'Houtse wel, ic saelt u lonen,
Dat ghijs u niet en selt becronen,
Na dat si u sijn ghelaten.
Men gheve hen der caritaten
Elcs daghes, om Gode.
Sint hier daghelijcs enen bode,
Die hen drincken hale ende eten.
Gheberst hen yet, laet mi weten.'
Die weduwe was vroo,
Dat haer comen was alsoo.

nor will I forget to tell you what happened to her two children, whom she left behind her in great need in the widow's house, with neither money nor food. I cannot describe to you their sorrow when they could not find their mother. The widow went to sit beside them, and she was filled with pity for them, and she said: 'I shall go to the abbess with these two children, and God will move her heart to be kind to them.' She put on their clothes and shoes and went with them to the convent, and she said: 'My lady, see now the destitution of these two poor creatures, terrified because their mother left them last night in my house. She has made off, I do not know whether to east or west, leaving the children desolate, and I should be glad to help them if I knew how.' The abbess said to her: 'Take good care of them and I shall reward you, so that you have no reason to regret that they have been left with you. Every day we shall give them our alms for the love of God. Send a messenger here daily to fetch food and drink for them, and if they need anything, let me know of it.' The widow was glad that things had happened so,

Si nam die kinder met hare
Ende hadder toe goede ware.
Die moeder, diese hadde ghesoghet
Ende pine daerom ghedooghet,
Haer was wel te moede,
Doen sise wiste in goeder hoede,
Haer kinder, die si begaf
In groter noot ende ghinc af.
Sine hadde vaer no hinder
Voort meer om hare kinder.
Si leide vort een heylech leven;
Menech suchten ende beven
Hadsi nacht ende dach,
Want haer die rouwe int herte lach
Van haren quaden sonden,
Di si niet en dorste vermonden
Ghenen mensche, no ontdecken,
Noo in dichten ooc vertrecken.

Hier na quam op enen dach
Een abt, diese te visenteerne plach
Eenwerven binnen den iare,
Om te vernemen oft daer ware
Enech lachterlike gherochte,
Daersi blame af hebben mochte[n].
Sdaghes als hire comen was,
Lach die sonderse ende las
Inden coor haer ghebet,
In groter twivelingen met.
Die duvel becorese metter scame,
Dat si haer sondelike blame
Vore den abt niet en soude bringhen.
Alsi lach inder bedinghen,
Sach si, hoe dat neven haer leet

and she took the children away with her, and took good care of them. The mother who had suckled them and suffered great sorrow on their account was glad when she learned that they were being well looked after, these children of hers whom she had left in great need and abandoned. She had no further fear or anxieties about her children, and she led a holy life, often sobbing and trembling, both night and day, when her heart was visited by contrition for her wicked sins, which she did not dare to tell or reveal to anyone, or to put down in writing.

Then, upon a certain day, there came an abbot, who was accustomed to visit the monostery once a year, to inquire whether there were any reprehensible rumours for which they might be to blame. On the day of his arrival, this sinful woman was kneeling in the choir and saying her prayers in great doubt. The devil was tempting her not to reveal her sinful guilt to the abbot for fear of shame. As she knelt and pondered, she saw

Een ionghelinc, met witten ghecleet;
Hi droech in sinen arm al bloot
Een kint, dat dochte haer doot.
Die ionghelinc warp op ende neder
Enen appel ende vinken weder
Voor tkint, ende maecte spel.
Dit versach die nonne wel,
Daersi in haer ghebede lach.
Si seiden: 'vrient, oft wesen mach,
Ende of ghi comen sijt van Gode,
Soo manic u bi sine ghebode,
Dat ghi mi segt ende niet en heelt,
Waerom ghi voor dat kint speelt
Metten sconen appel root,
Ende het leet in uwen arm doot?
U spel en helpt hem niet een haer.'
'Seker, nonne, ghi segt waer:
En weet niet van minen spele
Weder luttel no vele,
Hets doot, en hoort no en siet.
Al des ghelike en weet God niet,
Dat ghi leest ende vast:
Dat en helpt u niet een bast;
Hets al verloren pine,
Dat ghi neemt discipline:
Ghi sijt in sonden soo versmoort,
Dat God u beden niet en hoort
Boven in sijn rike.
Ic rade u: haestelike
Gaet ten abt, uwen vader,
Ende verteelt hem algader
U sonden, al sonder lieghen.
Laet u den duvel niet bedrieghen.
Die abt sal u absolveren

a young man dressed in white advancing towards her, and on his arm he carried a naked child, which seemed to her to be dead. The young man threw an apple up in front of the child and caught it again to amuse it. The nun, kneeling at prayer, saw this clearly, and she said: 'Friend, if it may be that you have come from God, I admonish you by your obedience to Him that you tell me without concealment why you are playing with that fine red apple in front of the child, when it is lying dead on your arm? There is nothing you can do for it by playing with it.' 'Certainly, nun, what you say is true. The child does not know anything about my play: it is dead, and can neither hear nor see. And in just the same way, God does not know about your prayers and fastings, and they do not help you in the least, and all your pains are wasted when you scourge yourself, for you are so overwhelmed by sin that God up in His realm does not hear your prayers. I counsel you to go quickly to the abbot, your spiritual father, and tell him the whole of your sins without any lies. Do not let the devil hoodwink you.

Vanden sonden, die u deren.
Eest, dat ghise niet wilt spreken,
God salse zwaerlike an u werken!'
Die ionghelinc ghinc ute haer oghen;
Hine wilde haer nemmeer vertoghen.
Dat hi seide, heeft si verstaen.
Smorghens ghinc si alsoo saen
Ten abt ende bat, dat hi hoorde
Haer biechte van worde te worde.
Die abt was vroet van sinne.
Hi seide: 'dochter, lieve minne,
Des en willic laten niet,
Bepeinst u wel ende besiet
Volcomelijc van uwen sonden.'
Ende si ghinc ten selven stonden
Den heyleghen abt sitten neven
Ende ontdecten hem al haer leven,
Ende haer vite van beghinne:
Hoe si met ere dulre minne
Becort was soo uter maten,
Dat si moeste ligghen laten
Haer abijt met groten vare
Eens snachts op onser vrouwen outare,
Ende rumede den clooster met enen man,
Die twee kindere aen hare wan.
Al dat haer ye was ghesciet,
Dies ne liet si achter niet;
Wat si wiste in haer herte gront,
Maecte si den abt al cont.
Doen si ghebiecht hadde algader,
Sprac dabt, die heyleghe vader:
'Dochter, ic sal u absolveren
Vanden sonden, die u deren,
Die ghi ji nu hebt ghelijt.

If you do not wish to speak now, God will take a heavy vengeance on you.' The young man vanished from her sight, nor did he ever appear to her again, but she understood what he had said, and first thing in the morning she went to the abbot and begged him to hear her out while she made her confession. The abbot was a prudent man; and he said: 'My dear daughter, let me hear you without delay. Reflect well and consider what have been all your sins.' And straightway she went to sit near the holy abbot, and she told him her whole life and story from the beginning: how the madness of love tempted her so excessively that one night, in great fear, she had abandoned her habit upon the altar of our Lady, and had fled from the monastery with a man, who had begotten two children upon her. She did not conceal anything which had ever happened to her, and she told the abbot everything which was in the depths of her heart. When she had made a full confession, this holy old man the abbot said: 'Daughter, I shall absolve you from the sins which have been afflicting you and which you have revealed to me.

Ghelooft ende ghebenedijt
Moet die moeder Gods wesen;'
Hi leide haer op thooft met desen
Die hant ende gaf haar perdoen.
Hi seide: 'ic sal in een sermoen
U biechte openbare seggen
Ende die soo wiselike beleggen,
Dat ghi ende u kinder mede
Nemmermeer, te ghere stede,
Ghenen lachter en selt ghecrigen.
Het ware onrecht, soudement swigen,
Die scone miracle, die ons here
Dede door siere moeder ere.
Ic saelt orconden over al.
Ic hope, datter noch bi sal
Menech sondare bekeren
Ende onser liever vrouwen eren.

Hi deet verstaen den covende,
Eer hi thuus weder wende,
Hoe ere nonnen was ghesciet;
Maer sine wisten niet,
Wie sie was, het bleef verholen.
Die abt voer Gode volen.
Der nonnen kinder nam hi beide
Ende vorese in sijn gheleide.
Grau abijt dedi hen an
Ende si worden twee goede man.
Haer moeder hiet Beatrijs.
Loof God ende prijs
Ende Maria, die Gode soghede,
Ende dese scone miracle toghede!
Si halp haer uut alre noot.
Nu bidden wi alle, aleine ende groot,

Praised and blessed be the Mother of God!' With these words he laid his hand upon her head and gave her absolution; and he said: 'I shall preach a sermon and reveal what you have told me in confession, but I shall disguise it so skilfully that neither you nor your children will ever suffer scorn. It would not be right to conceal in silence this fair miracle which our Lord has performed to the honour of His mother. I shall make it known everywhere, and I hope that it will serve to convert many sinners and to promote the honour of our blessed Lady.'

He made known to the convent before he returned home what had happened to one of their nuns, but none of them knew who she was, for that remained a secret. The abbot did as God commanded him, and took both the children of the nun into his protection. He clothed them both in the grey habit, and they became two good men. Their mother was called Beatrice. Praise and honour be to God, and to Mary, who suckled God and achieved this lovely miracle! She helped Beatrice in all her need, and now let us all, small and great,

Die dese miracle horen lesen,
Dat Maria moet wesen
Ons vorsprake int soete dal,
Daer God die werelt doemen sal.

Amen.

who listen to this miracle, pray that Mary be our intercessor in that fertile valley where God shall judge the world. Amen

MARY OF NIJMEGHEN

Prologue

In the time when Duke Arnold of Gelderland was imprisoned at Grave by his son, Duke Adolf and his fellow-conspirators, there was living three miles away from Nijmeghen a holy priest called Sir Gilbert, and with him there lived a pretty young girl called Mary, the daughter of his sister who had died. This girl kept house for her uncle, pleasing him greatly by her honesty and hard work.

How Sir Gilbert sent his niece Mary to Nijmeghen

It happened that this Sir Gilbert wanted to send his niece Mary into the town of Nijmeghen, to buy there the things which they needed, and he spoke to her thus:

THE UNCLE Mary!

MARY What is your pleasure, sir?

THE UNCLE Listen, child, and pay attention to what I say. You must go to Nijmeghen, to buy in the provisions which we need: candles, and oil for the lamp, vinegar, salt and onions, and sulphur sticks, as you have told me yourself. Here is the money, so go to Nijmeghen and buy what we need. Today is market day, all the better for you to find what you want.

MARY Sir, you know that I am ready to do your bidding in all obedience.

THE UNCLE It will be too late to come back home again tonight, because the days are now very short, and it is two good miles from here to Nijmeghen, and it is now ten o'clock or later. Listen, child: if it takes you so long that you think you cannot comfortably get home in daylight, stay the night there and I shall be easier in my mind.

Go and sleep at your aunt's my sister's; she will not turn you away for just one night, and I would rather that you did that than came home alone in the dark across the fields. There are far too many thieves about the road, and you are a pretty young creature, the sort they would use filthy language to.

MARY Sir, I shall do everything as you say, and nothing cotrary.

THE UNCLE My greetings to your anut, my sister, and now good-bye. See that you get good measure and weight in what we need.

MARY I shall, sir, good-bye.

THE UNCLE Good-bye Mary, my dear niece. May God's grace be always with you! Lord God, why is my heart so heavy? Is it because there is so much trouble here in the land, or is it because my niece has left me? How is it that I am so heavy-hearted? It is a strange thing, but just as the child went off, something which I do not understand came into my mind; and I thought that some mishap would come to her or to me. I wish that I had kept her at home! It is madness to allow young women or girls to walk about the countryside alone, for the world is full of crime.

How Mary was very unkindly received by her aunt

When Mary had taken leave of her uncle, she went to Nijmeghen, where she bought what she and her uncle needed. And on the very day on which she came to Nijmeghen, her aunt had quarrelled with four or five other women about Duke Adolf, who had put his father in prison, and she seemed more like a madwoman or a raging she-devil than a Christian, because she was on the side of the young Duke, and afterwards she destroyed herself when she learned that the old Duke had been freed from imprisonment by the help of the keeper of the castle at Grave, as you will presently hear. Mary, seeing that it was almost evening when she had done her errands, said to herself in this way:

Now I have had everything which we needed weighed and measured to my satisfaction, and I have bought and paid the proper price; but it seems to me that I have stayed so long that over there night is approaching fast. There is a sundial: what time can it be? Already it is half past four. I must stay here in the town tonight; there is only another hour of daylight left, and it will take me all of three hours to walk from here to my uncle's. No, I had far better stay. My aunt lives close by. I will go to her and ask her for a bed, and in the morning, as soon as I wake, I shall hurry back home and get to work. I can see my aunt standing outside her door. I shall go and greet her politely. Aunt, may Christ sweeten all your sorrows, and guard all those you love from harm.

THE AUNT Well, welcome to the devil: how are things in hell? Well, my fine lady, what do you want here?

MARY My uncle sent me when it was nearly noon to buy candles and mustard and vinegar and bitter essence and all the other things we needed at home, and by the time that I had been from one shop to the other and had found everything and bought it, it was so late; and you will not mind giving me a bed for the night, if you please. I would still go back home, but sometimes when it is dark a young girl can be watched and spied upon, and shamefully molested, and I am afraid of this.

THE AUNT Bless us and save us, you silly chit! For God's sake, are you so anxious about your virginity? My dear niece, it wasn't just yesterday that you found out how you were conceived, even if you are so coy about it now; and I do not think that it is only shopping that has kept you busy since noon.

MARY Truly, it was, Aunt.

THE AUNT You have been busy sitting somewhere in a corner drinking your fill. Niece, there are Tom and Dick and Harry who all know how to walk you country girls down into the cornfields, and when you play games in the evenings, Betty will always find a Jack to treat her. Yes, niece, you know all about it, for where you live there are plenty of lively lads.

MARY Why do you talk like this, Aunt?

THE AUNT Ah, you two-faced thing! Even if we must not say the truth, you have danced many a measure for which the piper was not paid in money. You may play this game for a long time yet: we are all virgins till our bellies swell.

MARY It wounds me to the heart that you should say such shameful things which I do not deserve.

THE AUNT I have talked to people who will swear that they have seen you doing things with your own uncle so shameless that it would be disgraceful for me to repeat them. You are bringing our whole family into disgrace. You will become a byword, you wretched creature, and I cannot bear to look at you.

MARY Oh, God, what sorrow is in my heart! The blood suddenly runs cold in all my body. To have to listen and to suffer guiltlessly such shameful words! Aunt, please tell me if you will let me have a bed, only for tonight and no longer.

THE AUNT I would rather seeing you lying as deep in the river Maas as the height of this house, to feed all the fish swimming in it. Be off from here before you are sorry! I am shaking like a leaf with rage.

MARY Aunt, what you say is most unjust.

THE AUNT Wait, this accursed bitch will not leave me in peace. Would you like me to pull down your plaits? She stirs up the maggots in my brain. I could lead the devil astray, I am in such an evil mood; I could tie him to a pillow as if he were a babe. I am in such a furious rage, I don't know whether I am on my head or my heels. I am in so foul a mood that everyone who meets me today will get the same answer that the devil gives his mother.

MARY Poor me, I am in for sad times. I stand here so amazed that I can give no account of myself. I am in such confusion I had best clear out of the town, even if there are thieves and footpads, and make a bed for myself under the leaves. I will ask no one else on earth for help, and if the devil himself came to me I would not trouble to speak to him. I shall sit down underneath this hedge; and I commend myself into God's hands, or else to the devil of hell.

How Mary left her aunt and went out of Nijmeghen

So this young girl Mary left her aunt, and went out of the town of Nijmeghen as night came on, weeping and very distressed, and walked on until she came to a great thick hedge. Then she sat down in great sorrow and wept and cried aloud, and often commended herself to the devil, saying to herself with sorrowful heart:

MARY Alas! weeping and crying and wringing my hands and calling myself accursed is now my only consolation. I have been shamefully used by my aunt, and can it be wrong for me to resent having such words to suffer when I have done no harm? Truly, no. Such resentment is growing in my heart that I sit here in evil mood, ready to curse myself everlastingly. Help! what temptations leap out upon me? Do I want to hang myself or cut my throat? Oh, youth, cannot you exercise control, cannot you act reasonably? How should I bear such words when I have not deserved them? I do not think that there is anyone living who could endure this without having earned it. I say all this in the despair which comes to afflict me. Come now to me and help me to lament, God or the devil, it is all the same to me.

The devil, who always spreads his traps and nets as he plots the damnation of souls, hearing these words said to himself as follows:

THE DEVIL These words commend this soul to me. I have already disguised myself as if I were a man, and all this is by the sufferance of God; and everything is as it should be, except for my one eye, and that is because of some spell. We evil spirits have not the power, nor can we obtain it, to make ourselves perfect human beings, under any condition. Always there has to be

195

something missing, in head or in hand or in foot. Now let me make my voice as sweet as I can, and speak so charmingly and gently that I do not scare this little darling. Gently does it with the women. Pretty child, why are you sitting here so forlorn? Has anyone harmed you, whether justly or not? I shall avenge you, as any decent fellow would. I cannot think that you have done any wrong, and therefore I offer myself as your comforter.

MARY God, help! Why am I so terrified? What is happening to me? I hardly can account for myself, but since I set eyes on this man, how faintly my heart is beating.

THE DEVIL Pretty child, do not fear any harm or sorrow. I shall do you no injury nor trouble you. But I promise you that if you will act by my advice and come with me, you may be sure that that before long I shall make you a lady of ladies.

MARY Friend, I am sitting here almost out of my mind, so upset and so discomposed by the scolding words that I have had to endure without any fault of mine—'whore, slut, bitch'—that I would as gladly entrust myself to the devil as to God, for I sit here half mad.

THE DEVIL By Lucifer, I cannot lose! She has swallowed down her draught of wrath, and now sits as if turned to stone by despair. I need not complain, for I may well hope to win. Pretty child, let me ask you if you will be my friend?

MARY Who are you, friend?

THE DEVIL A Master of Arts, and I never fail in what I undertake.

MARY It is all the same to me whom I go with: I'd as soon go with the worst as with the best.

THE DEVIL If you would give your love to me, I would teach you the arts as no one else could: the seven liberal arts, rhetoric, music, logic, grammar, geometry, arithmetic and alchemy, all of which are most important arts. There is no woman upon earth so proficient in them as I shall make you.

MARY You seem indeed to be a man full of art. Who are you then?

THE DEVIL What does that matter to you? It would be better for you not to ask me who I am. I am not the best of my family, but no one coul love you better than I.

MARY What is your name, friend?

THE DEVIL One-eyed Moenen; and I have lots of good friends who know me well.

MARY You are the devil out of hell.

THE DEVIL Whoever I am, I shall always be good to you.

MARY I feel no fear of you, no terror or horror. Though Lucifer himself were to come up out of hell, I should not run away from him. I am not touched by any fear.

THE DEVIL Well, my pretty, let us not waste time. If you will come with me and truly do my will, I shall teach you everything which you can possibly think of, as I told you before; and you will never again be without riches and jewels and money.

MARY That is well said, but whilst we are now talking, before you and I are joined in friendship, teach me the seven liberal arts, for I take great delight in all such things. You will teach them to me, won't you?

THE DEVIL You can trust me for that! I shall teach you everything you need to know.

MARY Necromancy, that is a fine art. My uncle knows a lot about it, and sometimes he does marvels which he gets out of a book. I do not think that he has ever failed. They say he can make the devil crawl through a needle's eye, whether he likes it or not. That is an art that I would like to learn.

THE DEVIL Pretty innocent, everything which I know is at your disposal, to make you happy; but I never learned necromancy, which is a very complicated and difficult art, in which are many dangers. If you were beginning to recite a spell with your pretty red lips, and you were to forget a word or a letter, so that you could not at once say the right thing to the spirit whom you had conjured, he would break your neck straight away. You can see how dangerous it is, my pretty flower.

197

MARY If that is the case, I shall not begin it: I do not want to learn anything which could kill me.

THE DEVIL Ah ha! that has put her off the scent! The idea of her wanting to learn necromancy! If she had learned necromancy, the danger would be in case she were to call up all hell and put them in danger, and even to exercise her powers over me if she chose, or get me into some tight place. I teach her necromancy? Not likely! I shall do what I can to make her forget the idea. Now listen to what I shall teach you, my pretty love, if you will just give necromancy up.

MARY What else shall I learn?

THE DEVIL I'll tell you now. I shall teach you all the languages in the world, so that the whole world will honour and pay tribute to you, for you have no idea what an achievement this is, and then, because you also know the seven liberal arts, you will be high in every man's esteem.

MARY The sorrows which oppress me lessen as I listen. I shall be most obedient to your will, if you will do this.

THE DEVIL Yet there is one other request I have to make of you, my pretty sweet. Do this for me and it will greatly benefit you.

MARY What request is that?

THE DEVIL That you will give up your name and take another from now on. 'Mary' is not a name I like to hear: there was once a Mary who did great harm to me and my friends, so that we have always disliked the name since then. Call yourself 'Lina' or 'Peggie' or 'Lizzie': do that, and before the year is out it will get you more than you ever had from your friends or relatives.

MARY Alas, why should this name displease you? It is the noblest and sweetest name in the world, and pleasing to everyone. 'Mary' or 'Maria', how could you hate this name? I will not take another name for all the world. I do not think that anyone could find a sweeter name.

THE DEVIL Indeed, I have just been wasting my time if I cannot make her change her name! Listen, my dear, if we are to go travelling together, you must change your name, however however little you may like it, or else we must part; and there is something else which you must promise me. Do not argue; a promise is a debt.

MARY What must I promise?

THE DEVIL That you will never again make the sign of the cross. Whatever happens, however much it may hurt you, you must not bless yourself.

MARY I will gladly promise. I do not attach great importance to the sign of the cross; but I cannot bear to deny my own name, for Mary, after whom I am called, is all my consolation and hope, and whatever sorrow or danger I am in, I call upon her at once for succour, and daily I honour her with the prayer that I learned as a child: 'Mary, Mary, be blessed by me.' As long as I have life, I shall never fail to do this; though I may go astray and live a bad life, I shall never forget to sing her praises.

THE DEVIL Well, if you are so attached to the name. I shall modify my wishes. I shall be satisfied for you to keep the first letter, the 'M' of your name; and so, dear lady, you shall be called 'Emma'. In your part of the world there are many girls and women called that.

MARY Very well, Moenen, since I cannot keep my own name, better let me be satisfied with the first letter than that we should part. Everywhere we go I shall be called 'Emma', although I do not like it.

THE DEVIL Yet be content: if you are not the mistress of all you long for within a year, I shall answer to you for it. Let us go to Bois-le-duc at once, and after that we shall have much to do. As soon as we please we may go to Antwerp, and there we shall give them all a surprise. Before we arrive there you will know all the languages you want to learn, as I promised you, and the seven liberal arts, as you required. Bastard and Malmsey will be your only drink; and if you keep my love and my gratitude,

you will achieve still more wonderful things. But finally I hope
that your soul will perish.

After these words Emma and Moenen set off for Bois-le-duc,
where they stayed for several days faring very well and paying
for each one of the people who came to eat or drink with them.
Now let us turn from Emma and Moenen, and speak about Sir
Gilbert, Emma's uncle. After Mary, whom we now call Emma,
had been absent for a few days, her uncle Sir Gilbert was very
surprised at her long absence, saying to himself as follows:

THE UNCLE Oh anxiety, crying so loudly inside me, how you
trouble my heart and mind and understanding, because Mary,
my niece, whom I sent to Nijmeghen marketing, has been
absent so long. It is true that I told her, if the night should
overtake her or if anything should alarm her, that she should
go to sleep at my sister's, because when I come to Nijmeghen
I always stay there. I shall have no happiness or peace of mind
until I know how she is. If some frightful thing were to have
happened to her, I should die hopeless and disconsolate, for
that child is all my consolation, and I reared her from her
infancy. I could not bear any harm to come to her; but young
girls are very easily led astray. I must go to Nijmeghen without
delay to get proper news of her. Bad news would be better
than no news.

With these words Sir Gilbert went to his sister's house to ask
about Mary, niece to him and to her aunt, who became very
angry and swore she knew nothing of her. At which he became
very sad and said to her thus:

THE UNCLE Alas, sister, you are deceiving me, telling me that
you know nothing about Mary.

THE AUNT My good man, I do not, believe me.

THE UNCLE Alas, sister, you are deceiving me.

THE AUNT I expect she'll be tucked away safe and sound, somewhere where roast chickens like her are had cheap.

THE UNCLE Alas, sister, you are deceiving me, telling me that you know nothing about her. You behave as if you are troubled and ill at ease, merely because I ask you quietly if you have seen her.

THE AUNT Of course I am troubled when you behave as if I had been responsible for her. It is eight or ten days ago since she came here, saying, 'Auntie, let me have a bed for tonight. I dare not go home for fear of being followed by thieves, the sort who like to ill-use young girls'; and I told her that she should go and lodge where she had been sitting drinking all day long.

THE UNCLE What? Had she been sitting drinking all day?

THE AUNT You can believe me, she had not been wasting her time, and she came here with a face as red as a well-thrashed backside, and when I told her what I thought of her, she nearly bit my head off, and she cleared off cursing and shouting, and that was the last I saw of my fine lady.

THE UNCLE Alas, what will become of me? O God in Trinity, where has the child gone?

THE AUNT My good man, she will have gone where there is plenty of drink, and plenty of boon companions.

THE UNCLE Alas, sister, it makes me weep to hear such words from you.

THE AUNT If you had locked her up in a box you could have saved yourself this trouble. Good heavens, my poor man, what harm is it going to do her if she does go her own way for a while? It will cost her nothing and do her no harm; she won't go round maimed for the rest of her life.

THE UNCLE Oh, it grieves me so to listen to you that I feel that my heart is breaking. I must turn around and wipe my eyes, for the tears are running down my cheeks. Oh, Mother of our Lord, whom I have visited at Aachen every year with great devotion, help me now in my need. And you, St Servatus, whose body lies at Maestricht, where each year I have caused many a fine light to be lit in devotion to you, I hope that now you will not fail me. When we are in need we must seek comfort from our friends. Now I shall have her searched for in every place, whether anyone has heard of her. Horrified as I am, it is no wonder though I grieve. No one is glad to be parted from what he loves.

After this Sir Gilbert left his sister with a sorrowful mind, because he had gained no news of his niece Mary.

How Mary's aunt cut her throat

In the meantime the keeper of the castle at Grave had released the old Duke Arnold from imprisonment and had conducted him to the town of Bois-le-duc, where he was hospitably received by the lord of the town. And when Mary's aunt heard of this, she became so angry in her venemous heart that she almost burst with spleen, saying:

THE AUNT Help, liver, lungs and spleen, teeth, heads, all is going badly for me. Anger will make me burst or melt, for I am swelling with spleen like a spider. I am going raging mad, I am losing my mind at the news which I have heard. That old thief who was safely locked up at Grave has been released and turned loose. This is the end of all my joys, for our young Duke, on whose side I am, will soon have the worst of it, I fear. This has so shaken me that I could easily give myself up, body and soul, and call all the devils that exist to come to my help.

THE DEVIL Ha ha, I ought to gain some profit out of this undertaking! This soul will be mine if I can spend just half an hour with her.

THE AUNT Is this not shameful?

THE DEVIL It is, and a great harm for those who are on the side of the young Duke.

THE AUNT Truly, who could it be who was not satisfied with so fine a fellow? Even if I have to burn in hell forever, I shall cut my throat out of spite, and so I shall be rid of these miseries. Oh, farewell, adieu, fine young prince! If you can rule again as duke, then it is nothing to me that I cut my life short. And so I stick this knife into my throat, and with this blow let me kill myself. Partizanship has destroyed many a soul.

THE DEVIL In the rabble of Hell, in endless torment shall I under Lucifer roast this soul. What fools they are, who for the sake of princes or lords destroy themselves out of partizanship. All who show themselves so obstinate end by being ours. Faction and strife provide Hell with many millions in the year, let him sorrow for it who will.

How Emma and Moenen travelled to Antwerp, where much harm came to the people through them

After Emma and Moenen had been at Bois-le-duc for some days, they set off for Antwerp and soon arrived there. And Moenen said to Emma thus:

MOENEN Now we are in Antwerp, where you wanted to be, and we shall have a great success here and live like princes. Let us go into The Tree for a pint of Rumney.

EMMA To The Tree, you say?

MOENEN Yes, love, and there you will see all the spendthrifts who waste their lives, all the daughters of joy and the whores who gamble with their lives. The freemen sit up above, the craftsmen below, and they all prefer to receive rather than give.

EMMA That is the life I love to see; nothing pleases me more.

MOENEN Let us have a drink in the Gold Room before we go, if you like. Sit down, love. Landlord, broach a new barrel: it would be a shame for it to go sour.

THE POTBOY What wine would you like, sir?

MOENEN A pint of Grenade, and a pint of Ypocras for my wife, and a pint of Rumney. There's nothing like it for warming you up; it raises your spirits, however low they are.

THE POTBOY You're right, and here it is, a broach, a broach; the very best, the very best, and good measure.

FIRST DRINKER Look, Jack, there's a fine wench over there.

SECOND DRINKER True, and an ugly-looking devil with her.

FIRST DRINKER Let us take our drink over to them and if we find out that she is only his strumpet, we'll have her for ourselves.

SECOND DRINKER Tonight he can sample my knife, because he's an ill-favoured lout, but the girl is as pretty as can be. If she's only his whore, she is mine tonight. Will you help me?

FIRST DRINKER I swear I will; and I will stick close to your side. God bless you, friend!

MOENEN Come and drink with us, good fellows!

SECOND DRINKER No, friend, we have plenty here, but may we come and sit with you?

MOENEN Yes, and sit as long as you like. Good company does me no harm.

FIRST DRINKER Excuse me, where do you two come from?

MOENEN From Bois-le-duc or thereabouts.

EMMA Moenen dear, would it be through geometry if I were to be able to count exactly how many drops of wine there are in a pot?

MOENEN Yes, dear, but have you remembered how to do it? That was something I taught you yesterday.

EMMA That is true, indeed, and you also taught me logic, and I have remembered all that as well.

A DRINKER Friend, what is that your wife says? Can she really calculate exactly how many drops of wine went into this pot? I have never heard anything to equal it.

MOENEN That is nothing to some of the things she can do. You never saw the like of her in all your life. She understands all the seven liberal arts, astronomy and geometry, arithmetic, logic and grammar, music and rhetoric, the most ancient of them all. She could hold her own against the cleverest scholar who studied in Paris or Louvain.

THE SECOND DRINKER My good friend, I beg you to allow us to see or hear something of her skill.

THE FIRST DRINKER Yes, please, and I will buy you each a pint of wine, and I swear that if anyone tries to interrupt you, we shall fight them for you, if they give you trouble.

MOENEN The poem you made up yesterday when we were walking in the High Street at noon, say that for them.

EMMA Please excuse me. I am a very dull scholar at rhetoric, much as I should like to practise it, so as to master all the seven liberal arts; it requires more than industry for rhetoric, which is an art which must come of its own accord. All the other arts can be learned by application and instruction, if one will work hard at them, but rhetoric is to be esteemed above them all. It is a gift of the Holy Spirit, and though one finds many ignorant creatures who despise it, that gives great sorrow to lovers of rhetoric.

THE SECOND DRINKER Well, my dear, how many times do you want us to ask you?

THE FIRST DRINKER Recite something for us that you know: it is only for fun, and we shall be satisfied, and then I shall recite something too.

EMMA Then be quiet, and I shall sing you a song as well as I can; rhetoric has to be listened to and taken in, so do not let let us have any chattering.

O rhetoric, o true and lovely art, I who have always esteemed thee above all, I lament with grief that there are those who hate you and despise you. This is a grief to those who love you. Fie upon those who count you merely folly. Fie upon them who do so, for I wholly despise them. But for those who support you, life is full of hurt and sorrow. Ignorant men are the destruction of art.

They say in the proverb that through art grows the heart, but I say that it is a lying fable, for should some great artist appear, those who are unskilled and know not the first thing about art will make their opinion prevail everywhere, and artists will be reduced to beggary. Always it is the flatterer who is preferred, and always artists suffer such harm, and ignorant men are the destruction of art.

Fie upon all crude, coarse, common minds, trying to measure art by your standards: everyone should pay honour to pure art, art which is the ruler of many a pleasant land. Honour be to all who are the promoters of art, fie upon the ignorant who reject art, for this is why I proclaim the rule that ignorant men are the destruction of art.

Prince, I will devote myself to art, and do everything in my power to acquire it. But it is to all lovers of art a sorrow that ignorant men pay so little honour to art.

Many people assembled to listen to this poem, and seeing this, Moenen showed his cunning, and organized such an uproar that one of the company was stabbed to death, and he who did it had his throat cut. So Emma and Moenen lived at The Golden Tree in the market place, where every day, through their instrumentation, murders and killings and other evil deeds were done. And Moenen had great joy of this, saying to himself thus:

THE DEVIL What marvels I can perform! I hope that Hell will gain some profit from it. If I am in charge here for a while, I shall thrust still more down into the mouth of Hell. It would be a pity for us to leave this inn, for all who come here to spend their time, tricksters, duellers, profligate strumpets, pimps, whoremongers, are all found in great plenty; and they are the sort of people who bring me profit. So I must stay where I am in this house. I shall go at once and ask the landlord what he will charge for the two of us. If I lodge here, I shall have everything here which I require just as I want it, and if there is any secret into which I can pry, I shall always seek to stir up strife. In this next year I shall have a hundred stabbed to death, for Lucifer to welcome into the pleasure-gardens of Hell. I shall disguise myself as a quack, so that everyone will esteem me, and I shall say that I know how to lead people to hidden treasure, for which great honour will be paid to me. I shall know just how to describe all the events which have happened to men. Before a month is out people will be following me by the thousand because of my arts, and I shall gain riches as no man ever did. My dear Emma will love me more and more, and if the Almighty does not hinder me, I shall before a year is past trap more than a thousand souls. But should it be His will, all my work will have been in vain.

How Emma began to lament her sinful life

So Emma, living in Antwerp and seeing that she was leading a very evil and sinful life, because for her sake Moenen was every day the cause of very much harm, said to herself thus:

EMMA O memory and understanding, if you were to think upon the life which I am living now, it would seem sinful and foul to you. I have forsaken the light of Heaven, and I walk the road to Hell, which is very hideous. I see and observe how nearly every day someone here is injured or killed because of me, and I know well that it is this man Moenen who is the cause of this harm. And he is a bad lot, and this is the root of it. I feel it strongly, though he does not himself say it straight out, that he must be a devil or little better. Oh, Aunt, those great and cruel reproaches of yours will make me into a damned whore, eternally expelled from the grace of Almighty God. Alas, the most lamentable part of my situation is that I have gone too far, however much I may wish to turn back. Once

I used to serve Mary every day with my prayers or some other service pleasing to her, but now my devotion is all gone, and Moenen would not endure it, for he will not suffer me even to make the sign of the cross. By that one can feel that he is evil, when he shuns the cross's blessing. Consider how I could possibly repent—things have gone too far now for repentance! Aha! there are two fellows over there who stood me a drink yesterday. I'll go over to them and wet my whistle.

And with this she went to sit and drink with her boon companions, and Moenen so contrived it that one of them got his death. And the one who did it was led by Moenen outside the town, where he murdered another man by counsel of Moenen, who had told him that the man he murdered had much money, for which he ought to kill him. At which Moenen was very glad, saying:

THE DEVIL With the aid of Lucifer's traps and the pit of Hell, how I am destroying these people every day! They think that I am a fine lord, and I know just what to say to take them in, and so they all come flocking after me. I know how to give them clear advice, and so I whisper to the women how to drive men mad for love of them, or I tell them how to feed them so they do not live another week. I have done this more than once, and Lucifer has not lost one of them, believe me. And now I am beginning to teach people how to find hidden treasure; and only yesterday it cost one of them his life. I told him where there was a treasure hidden and growing mouldy, in a stable, underneath a beam on which the whole weight of the stable was resting. I told him that he would have to dig deep into the ground, and he would find pound upon pound of the hidden treasure. At once he started to dig there, but as soon as he had dug so far that he undermined the beam and the posts supporting it, the beam fell to the ground and crushed this poor idiot under it! This is nothing to what I shall do soon, if I am not hindered from on high. They will believe that I am a god, and I shall lead them down into Hell in troops.

After Emma and Moenen had lived at The Golden Tree in Antwerp for about six years, and an astonishing amount of harm had been caused by them, Emma began to long to visit her uncle and her other dear ones in Gelderland, and to ask Moenen to allow her to do this and to travel with her. To which he replied:

THE DEVIL Emma, I do not refuse what you ask. Do you want to visit your friends, you say?

EMMA I do ask you for this, if it were your pleasure.

THE DEVIL Dear one, I do not forbid it.

EMMA I have not seen my aunt at Nijmeghen or my uncle at Venloo for six or seven years.

THE DEVIL That is why I do not refuse you. Certainly, let us go to visit your friends.

EMMA Those who were nearest to me do not know where I went, any more than if the ground had swallowed me up. And my uncle thought the world of me; I know that he has shed many a tear for me.

THE DEVIL That old hypocrite's prayers have often hindered me, when I should have liked to break every bone in her body. I should have broken her neck long ago, but his prayers to that woman all in white have always stopped me. I never once was able to get the opportunity I wanted.

EMMA What do you say, Moenen?

THE DEVIL Nothing, Emma my dear. I give you permission, just as you ask, to see your friends as you wish to. So go now and pay our account with the landlord at The Tree, where we have been lodging, and tomorrow we shall go to your uncle's, or to your other friends, wherever you take me. I am quite ready.

EMMA I shall go and ask how much is still outstanding on our bill, and pay it all.

THE DEVIL Do that, my darling, pay everything they ask, down to the last halfpenny. I can be sure that I am not going to lose by this, when we go to her uncle the parson's. Just let me catch him once off his guard, and I shall have it all my own way. Then I shall break the hypocrite's neck, for if he were once out of the way, the girl would be wholly in my power. But whatever I plan or say, it is all in vain if the Almighty does not give me His full consent: I cannot touch a hair of his head against God's will.

How Emma and Moenen went to Nijmeghen

So Emma and Moenen went to Nijmeghen, where they arrived in time for the Rogation Day procession; and Emma was very glad, and Moenen said to her thus:

THE DEVIL Well, Emma, here we are, just as you asked me, in Nijmeghen, and today is Rogation Day, too. You said that your aunt used to live here. Do you not want to go to visit her?

EMMA To go to visit her is one thing, but I would not dream of asking her for shelter, or any food or drink. She would only give me shameful language and furious anger, as she did once before with no hesitation. It was what she said in her folly and ignorance which led me first to this life of shame that I am leading now, alas!

THE DEVIL I hardly think you need to go there, my dear, my joy. It is time that you know that your aunt has been dead for three years.

EMMA What do you say? Dead?

THE DEVIL Yes, dearest heart.

EMMA How do you know that, Moenen?

THE DEVIL I know it for certain.

EMMA This is a great sorrow to me.

THE DEVIL Truly, it is.

EMMA Wait, what do I see over there? Let us watch before we go away. Look, look, a great crowd of people is gathering. Is something happening? Go and ask someone quickly.

THE DEVIL No, love, they are just going to play a pageant on wheels.

EMMA That happens every year on this day. Now that I remember, this is the play of Mascaron. I cannot tell you how good it is. My uncle always used to come to see it. Oh, Moenen, let us stay and listen to it.

THE DEVIL It is all a lot of nonsense. Do you really want to listen to such drivel? We had far better go look for a roast and some wine.

EMMA Oh, Moenen, it is always so good. There were times when I heard my uncle say that this play is better than all the sermons ever preached. Such plays often contain very good stories. My darling, if it would not bore you I should like to see it.

TE DEVIL I do not want to agree. By Lucifer's backside, I am very frightened! If she were to hear something in the play so forceful that she were seized with remorse or suspicion, by Lucifer, all my great plans would be useless.

EMMA Oh, Moenen, let me listen to it!

THE DEVIL Well, only till I tell you to come away, or I shall be angry.

Emma tormented Moenen so long, asking him to let her listen to the play, that in the end he agreed, but very grudgingly, as you have heard. And the play began as follows:

MASCARON Hallo, here I am, Mascaron, Lucifer's advocate at law, come to plead my case before the Omnipotent Judge Himself, to ask Him why He shows more mercy and grace to the miserable human race than to us, poor spirits whom He has everlastingly rejected. Even if a human being had committed all the sins by himself which all the men in the world commit, if he has a good and heartfelt contrition and a good intention, he will attain mercy, but we poor spirits, who never sinned except by one brief thought, have because of it been cast into the abyss, without hope, into everlasting cruel torment. I, Mascaron, procurator of Lucifer, demand once more of You, God of mercy, why You have denied mercy to us more than to man, who daily commits unspeakable sins.

GOD My mercy is withheld from no man who feels contrition before the end of his life, and who acknowledges, while there is yet time, that I am a merciful and just God. But those who persist in their shameful ill-doing, who never feel the qualms of conscience, they must sink down with Lucifer into the abyss, where there will be nothing but lamentation.

MASCARON In many respects Your justice is imperfect, even though they call You a God just in all His ways. In the days of Abraham and Moses and David men could call You just, because then they saw You blaming and condemning and punishing men for a single unclean thought; but nowadays, even if a child were to rape its own mother, to strike its father down or tread him underfoot, or if one brother were to accuse another of every evil ever committed, if he has heartfelt contrition, at once he gains Your mercy.

GOD Why did I die a death so disgraceful, so shameful, lifted up on the Cross, unless to obtain for every man, young and old, My Father's grace?

MASCARON On this account You ought to be more angry and stern than You were before: naked, You died so shameful a death, so as to cleanse human nature; and yet men are more hardened than they were before in their horrible, disgraceful sins. One cannot describe them or conceal them. Reasonable men shudder when they reflect that things which men under the Old Law dared not think of, men today do without fear.

GOD What you say is true, Mascaron. People are now so hardened in evil-doing that unless they will turn away from it, I shall punish them with the strokes of My mighty sword of justice, and send down My plagues which are cruel to suffer.

OUR BLESSED LADY Oh my child, if You condemn man to punishment with plague, that will greatly afflict me. Let Yourself be entreated, leave mankind in peace for yet a little while. Send signs or warnings to the people first, as You have done before under such constraint: earthquakes or double suns or stars with tails, so that they can understand from such tokens that You are immeasurably angered. Then perhaps they will forsake their sins for fear lest they are more afflicted.

GOD No, Mother, you waste your labours. Again and again I have sent such tokens, which ought to have struck terror into their hearts: pestilences, wars, famines, which should have made men to eschew the sins which offend My Divinity. But the more they have been afflicted, the more they have gone astray, never thinking of everlasting death, full of lamentation. All they ever say is: 'Why should I trouble? One act of contrition at the end, and God, who is merciful, will have mercy on me.'

Emma, listening to the play, began to reflect with sorrowful heart upon her sinful life, saying to herself:

EMMA Lord God, how am I moved, listening to this pageant? I hear such reasons and arguments that I am filled with pure contrition and remorse.

THE DEVIL Well, are we going to stay here all day? You, speak! What do you want to listen to this drivel for? Dear one, let us go.

EMMA No, it is no use shouting and tugging and pulling at me. As long as this play lasts, you will not move me from here—let those go who want to. This is better than a sermon.

THE DEVIL Lucifer's backside, help me! It is a torment to me to let her stand here. She will catch contrition, I think, if she stands here listening to all this prating. I shall wait a little longer, but if she will not come away I shall give her a good punching and get her away like that.

So Moenen would gladly have prevented Emma from listening to the play, but she stayed and heard it, whether he liked it or not. And the play continued so:

MASCARON O guide of the heavens and of the elements, God throned on high in your justice, would You not permit and consent to Lucifer and his minions in Hell that we might chastize men for their misdeeds and their great wickedness? Otherwise You will never have an end to the evils in which they persist: Your hand of justice must chastize them, if You are to be acknowledged among mankind.

GOD Mascaron, I shall give consent for mankind to be afflicted, because nothing instils fear into them, unless they feel a knife at their throats.

OUR BLESSED LADY O Son, mankind will improve in every way. Do not be too hasty in unleashing Your punishments. Think of the breasts that You sucked, think of the womb in which You lay, think of the Passion You suffered, think of Your bloody sweat in Your anguish. Was not all this for the sake of man? Was it not so that he might attain to Your Father's mercy? You have said this Yourself, so what will You do now? If one man had committed all the sins of the world, if he uttered one heart-felt cry for Your mercy, he would be received with open arms. This is what You said, and many a man knows it.

GOD That is what I said, and I am not sorry for it, my Lady Mother, and I say again that though a man had committed every sin which one could imagine, if he calls upon Me with contrition, he shall be one of My chosen. And rather than that one soul should be lost, I would suffer all My torments again twice over which the Jews inflicted upon Me in days long past. O man, think well upon these things!

How Emma went on listening to the play, so that she repented even more of her sins, saying thus:

EMMA Now at last   the tears begin to run fast down over my face. Oh, what compunction have I felt, as I heard these words, oh Lord of lords! Could it be possible that if I were to repent I could attain to Your grace? I never suspected it until now. Could it be possible? I never thought so before. I have too gladly consented to what I have done, foolishly taking pleasure in my own wilful acts. Oh, earth, open and swallow me up, for I am not fit to tread upon you.

THE DEVIL Help, Modicat, my eyes grow fiery with rage! This girl is getting a bellyful of repentance. Let us go off to some pleasant part of the town and drink a pot of wine.

EMMA Leave me alone, and get away from me, you evil, cruel devil! Alas for me that it was you whom I summoned and called to, forgetting You who are divine and merciful. Oh, oh, I am filled with such heartfelt remorse that my heart will crack! Oh, I am dying, my strength is failing me!

THE DEVIL Lucifer's liver and lungs and spleen, help me! Now may I well curse and shoot flames from my eyes and howl, for all my plans are going astray. What I have achieved will be little esteemed among the revellers in Hell. Get up, in the name of every devil, or I will carry you off as you are to fry in Hell!

EMMA Oh Lord, have mercy on me!

THE DEVIL Oh, indeed? Now I can hear remorse pulling at her placket! I will carry her off high above the roofs into the sky, and throw her down from there. If she ever draws breath again that will be her good fortune, the ugly wretch! Come   on, come on, you are coming up into the sky with me.

After these words Moenen the devil lifted Emma up into the air, higher than any house or church, so that her uncle and all the people saw this, which greatly astonished them, not knowing what it could mean.

How Moenen threw Emma down from on high, and how her uncle recognized her

When Moenen the devil had carried Emma high up above all the houses, he threw her down into the street from above, intending to break her neck, which greatly terrified the people. And Sir Gilbert, her uncle, who was also listening to the play, was amazed to think what this could mean and how it was possible that anyone could fall from so high up, saying and asking one of those standing near him as follows:

THE UNCLE If she has not broken her neck, that is her good fortune. There is unspeakable terror in my heart, as I see all the people looking at this person. Do I not know her? Who is the woman?

A CITIZEN I want to see if I know her, but the people are crowding around her so that no one can get near her. Follow me, sir, and I shall make a way for us. If anyone thinks that I do not know how to push, he is wrong. Here you are, sir, the girl is lying here unconscious, all alone.

THE UNCLE That is not surprising. Help, I could swear that there is no drop of blood left in all my body! The tears start from my eyes. My veins dry up, my face is white. I have never felt myself so weak. Oh, my friend, please look after me, I beg you.

THE CITIZEN Wait, what is the matter with you, sir? You are so changed you seem as if you were a dead man.

THE UNCLE In this moment of horror I could wish to die. Oh, Atropos, come and put out my light!

THE CITIZEN Why are you lamenting like this?

THE UNCLE Oh, this is my niece! I have already suffered enough on her account. This is she whom I have been seeking for over

216

seven years, and now, alas, here she is lying with her neck broken. Oh, earth, open and swallow me up! No longer do I wish to stay here.

THE CITIZEN Are you sure that it is she?

THE UNCLE Could I fail to recognize her? Or do you think that I am out of my mind?

THE DEVIL Help, all you ministrants of hellish joys: I could piss on my own tail out of sheer rage. I cannot think what to do in this business. This is her uncle: how shall I contrive it now? I could have easily broken her neck, but the prayers of this pious parson have stood in my way. If I only had the power I would carry him off to Hell this instant.

THE CITIZEN Look, sir, I see her moving.

THE UNCLE If she would move, that would be the cure for much of my suffering. It is true, she is indeed moving.

EMMA Oh, what has happened to me? Where have I been, and where am I now? Oh, Lord, am I still in Your favour, so that I may attain to grace? Yes, truly, I am, for had You not taken me into Your omnipotent protection, I should have been thrust down for ever into eternal torment, banished body and soul from the Kingdom of the Lord.

THE UNCLE If you can still speak, Mary, my niece, speak to me, who have sighed so many sighs for you and made so many laments, and asked for you high and low! And now I find you, in the middle of this crowd, and in this wretched state.

EMMA Oh, is it you, my uncle? Oh, if only God would grant that I could now be in the same state as I was when I last saw you, that I had never gone away! Oh, when I think of what I am, I am sure that I shall be everlastingly damned!

THE UNCLE Niece, what you say is sinful, for no one is lost except him who gives himself up for lost. Why should you be damned? That would be a dreadful thing. But how do you come to be here? That is what I greatly want to know. A moment ago you were up there in the sky. Please tell me how this could be. I do not know that I have ever seen anyone so high up before.

EMMA Uncle, it would be impossible for me to give you a reasonable account of all my adventures. Once I surrendered myself wholly to the devil, and then I kept company with him for some seven years. I cannot describe it all to you; I shall just tell you as briefly as I can how I have lived and what we have done during those seven years. They could indeed write books about it. There is no evil to compare with the evil I have done. But, at the end of all these strange events, I came back here to our own country to visit my friends, and as we passed through the town here and came into the market place, I saw the play about Mascaron being performed, and I approached to listen, and from the words I heard I was seized with such contrition that it angered him who was with me, and he carried me off up to where all the people saw me, high up in the sky.

THE UNCLE Alas, alack, is this true, niece? Was the devil with you?

EMMA Yes, Uncle, and he has been with me now for about seven years, since I first put myself at his command and began to go around with him.

THE UNCLE Help us, almighty God! To hear this fills my whole being with horror. We must drive this spirit away from you, if you are ever to attain to God's blessed kingdom.

THE DEVIL Ah, you hypocrite, that you cannot do; you cannot separate me from her. If I want to I shall carry her off, skin and bones and all, and take her to where they do not stint the sulphur and the pitch.

THE UNCLE Will you, you evil spirit?

THE DEVIL Yes, I will, you whoreson hypocrite! She is mine, she has surrendered herself to me, she has forsaken Almighty God and she has bound herself to me, and so she must burn in the fires of hell; and if you were to try to snatch from me what is my possession, I would break every bone in your body.

218

THE UNCLE Evil spirit, I shall stand in your way. Here in my breviary I have eight or ten lines written on a piece of paper, and they will soon make you laugh on the other side of your face.

THE DEVIL Oh, oh! My hackles rise, my hair stands on end, as he reads it there. What shall I do now? By Modicat, if I lose this woman now, I shall be flogged with whips of fire. I grind my teeth for very rage, and I blow sparks from the fires of hell out of my ears and cheeks! All men can now see from me that we are less than powerless when what we plan is displeasing to the Almighty Lord. I think that this soul and I must now part.

THE UNCLE Let us go, Mary my niece, and I shall take you to the deacon's, and have a fire lit for you. I think that you must be injured in every limb, since he took you up so high and let you fall down. You must be badly hurt.

EMMA I pay no heed to it at all. Uncle, I am willing to suffer ten thousand times this pain, for which there may be no cure at all, and more than any pen could write; if only God's mercy be not withdrawn from me, I do not care what becomes of me, if I may have His consolation and grace.

THE UNCLE Do not let this resolution weaken, and I can assure you that you will gain what you wish for—the Kingdom of God. Daily we read in the Scriptures that to attain to God's perfect glory, nothing is needed more than a perfect final contrition.

After this, Sir Gilbert went with his niece to all the most learned priests in the town of Nijmeghen; but no priest, however learned, however experienced, however holy or devout, once he had understood the case, dared in any way be so bold as to absolve her or impose on her any penance for her sins, which were so dreadful and so unnatural; and so they were all greatly oppressed.

How Sir Gilbert travelled to Cologne with his niece

On the following day, very early in the morning, Sir Gilbert prepared himself as if he were about to celebrate Mass, and, taking the glorious, blessed and holy Sacrament in his hand, he set off with his niece Emma for Cologne. And Moenen the devil followed them from far off, but he did not dare to approach them or to come near to Emma, because of the might of the Holy Sacrament. Yet at times he would throw a split oak or some other tree after them, to break both their necks. But our Blessed Lord would not permit this, because Emma was accustomed every day to say a prayer in honour of our Blessed Lady. So in the end they had travelled so long and so far that they arrived at Cologne, where Emma made her confession to the Bishop. But she obtained no counsel for this, because her sin was so unnatural and so great that he had no power to absolve her from it.

How Emma and her uncle travelled to Rome, and how Emma made her confession to the Pope

After this, Emma and her uncle left the Bishop and travelled from Cologne to Rome, where they arrived after much travelling and great labour. And Emma said her confession before the Pope, saying with weeping eyes:

EMMA Oh viceregent of God, yes, God upon earth, as men teach us, the earth has not upon it a greater sinner than I, who am, I believe, eternally excluded from the heavenly Kingdom.

THE POPE Why is that, my child?

EMMA I am the devil's mistress, and I have been for more than seven years. I talked with him, walked with him, went with him where we pleased. Understand this matter well. I have done with him that which man and wife do. Have I not reason to feel horror at myself?

THE POPE What, my child, with the devil of Hell?

EMMA Yes, Holy Father!

THE POPE And did you know well when he came to you that it was the devil?

EMMA Yes, I did, and that is why I mourn!

THE POPE But how could you have commerce with the devil when you knew who he was?

EMMA Father, it was the good times, all the money and the presents which he gave me, you must know this, which made me do it, and now it makes me shudder. There was nothing which came into my mind which he did not give to me as I desired. And the worst of all, which afflicts me most and sends the greatest anguish to my heart, is that so many men lost their lives in the places which we frequented. More than two hundred, Holy Father, have been murdered and sent to their deaths for my sake, at one time or another.

THE POPE Help us, oh divine Lord! For such misdeeds you must indeed now life a live of sorrow.

EMMA Oh, Father, give me counsel, if that is possible, and lay penance on me before we part. I do not care how heavy it is.

THE POPE I hardly dare try so greatly the mercy of our Lord. For you to have lived with the devil! Never have such sins been confessed to me before, and then, more, that so many lives have been lost because of your vicious ways! I do not know what penance to give you which would be heavy enough for such sinful deeds. For you to have been with the devil—it is too beastly! Oh God, unfathomable well of grace, give me counsel in this matter, for my own mind is wholly oppressed. Oh righteous Judge, pour into me Your inspiration, out of Your great glory. Wait—it comes to my mind—it would be a great sorrow to me to reject you. Call the priest who came with you, and he shall hear what your penance is.

EMMA Where are you, uncle?

THE UNCLE I have been standing here at the door, full of sorrow and fear until I know what is to happen.

THE POPE Then listen to my decision. It would be a sorrow to me, and it would be pitiful, for anyone to be lost if one could prevent it, nor would God gladly suffer it. Look there, at those three iron rings. The biggest of them you must lock round her neck, and the other two, without further delay, fasten tight and firm round her arms; and she must wear the rings until they wear through or fall off of their own accord. Then will all her sins have been forgiven her, and not until then will she be freed and quit.

THE UNCLE I think that it will be a very long time before they fall off by themselves, for they are so thick and heavy and hard. In a hundred years not a quarter of their thickness would wear away.

THE POPE She may so free herself in complete and heartfelt penance of her sins that they may themselves fall from her arms and neck. But they must be firmly fastened on.

THE UNCLE Good, Father, I shall have them fastened on so well and so firmly that they will never fall off, unless it be the work of God. Oh, you who are priest and cleric over all ranks, by your favour we will now leave you, and travel our own road back to our country, whence we came.

THE POPE May the Almighty, He who has reconciled us all, make your sufferings as sweet as they are prolonged.

EMMA Farewell, Holy Father!

THE POPE Go in God's keeping, daughter, and be resolute in your penance, for on high, in heaven's bliss, perfect penance is highly esteemed, and penance can cure many ills, more than all the other remedies of which we read.

So Emma received her penance from the Pope. And at once her uncle had the rings fastened so firmly around her neck and her arms that they would not have come off all her lifetime, had it not been by the consent and the miraculous intervention of our Blessed Lord.

How Emma left Rome, and how she became a nun in the house for converted sinners at Maestricht

When Emma had the rings on, as you have heard, she left the city of Rome with her uncle, and they travelled on until they came to Maestricht, where Emma became a nun in the convent of converted sinners, and her uncle helped her in this. And after he had helped her in this matter, he took his leave of her and travelled to his own territory, where he lived for another twenty-four years, after he had helped his niece to enter the convent, and as long as he lived he visited her once a year.

How the angel of God took the rings off Emma's neck and hands

When Emma resided in the convent of which we have written, she lived so holy a life and performed such great penances that the merciful Christ forgave her all her sins, sending His angel to her, where she lay and slept, who took off her rings. At which Emma was very joyful, saying:

EMMA The long nights are seldom welcome to those whose hearts are oppressed with grief and heaviness. Their sleep is great disquiet or greater sorrow, with grievous dreams terrifying them with further terrors. Many such troubles come to me, and who shall tell me the true meaning of my dreams which have come to me as I lay? I thought that I was taken out of the fires of Hell, and borne up from there into Heaven, and many white doves came flying towards me, who with their wings struck off my bonds. Wait, what is this I see, O God full of blessings! Have I attained to this great grace? Yes, truly I have, my bonds are off, as I can see, and they lie here beside me! This is the work of God, of You who are our powerful shield and defence against our weakness! Never can I pay proper thanks to You for this. Oh man, full of misdeeds and sins, from this you can take example, and say eternal praises to Almighty God in honour of this unparalleled goodness. In your own poor and feeble way, pay fitting honour to Him in His temple.

The Epilogue

So, God's chosen friends, this happened once long ago, and it is true, though many think it a lie; and if you went to Maestricht, to the house of converted sinners, you would see Emma's grave, and over the grave the three rings hanging, and under the rings, written in letters still legible, the story of her life and of the penance which she suffered, and how and when it happened. These are the signs which convince me that it it true. She lived some two years more, after her rings fell off, it was told to me, always performing penances and exercises to gain the favour of the King of kings. Accept this thankfully and without complaint, this poor story, for it was written for love, that we may receive heavenly glory. Amen.

WALTHAM FOREST PUBLIC LIBRARIES

BIBLIOGRAPHY

Beatrice of Nazareth: *There are Seven Manners of Loving*
L. Reypens, S. J., and J. van Mierlo, S. J.: *Beatrijs van Nazareth, Seven manieren van minne critisch uitgegeven* (Louvain, 1926)

Hadewijch of Antwerp: *Letters*
J. van Mierlo, S. J.: *Hadewijch, Brieven*. Vol. 1, Text and Commentary (Antwerp, 1947)
F. van Bladel. S. J., and B. Spaapen, S. J.: *Hadewijch, Brieven* (Lannoo, 1954)
J.-B. P(orion): *Hadewych d'Anvers* (Paris, 1954)

Blessed John Ruysbroek: *The Book of the Sparkling Stone*
L. Reypens, S. J., and M. Schurmans, S.J.: *Werken*, Vol. 3 (Malines, 1932)
Bazire, Joyce, and Colledge, Eric: *The Chastising of God's Children and The Treatise of Perfection of the Sons of God* (Oxford, 1957)
Colledge, Eric: *The Spiritual Espousals* (London, 1952)

Beatrice
Barnouw, A. J.: *Beatrijs, a Middle Dutch legend* (London, Publications of the Philological Society, 1914)

Mary of Nijmeghen
A. L. Verhofstede and others: *Mariken van Nieumeghen* (second edition, Antwerp, 1951)
H. M. Ayres and A. J. Barnouw: *Mary of Nimmegen* (Cambridge, Mass. 1932)

General
S. Axters, O. P., translated D. Attwater: *The Spirituality of the Low Countries* (London, 1954)
S. Axters, O. P.: *Geschiedenis van de Vroomheid en de Nederlanden*

(Vol. 1, until c. A. D. 1300, Antwerp, 1950: Vol. 2, the Age of Ruysbroek, Antwerp, 1953)

Romana Guarnieri: *Marguerite Porete, La mirouer des simples ames* (Rome, 1961)

H. Grundmann: *Religiöse Bewegungen im Mittelater* (Berlin, 1935)

C. Henriquez: *Quinque Prudentes Virgines* (Antwerp, 1630)

A. Mens: *Oorsprong en betekenis van de nederlandse begijnen begarden beweging* (Louvain, 1947)

T. Weevers: *Poetry of the Netherlands in its European context*, 1170-1930 (London, 1960)

BIBLIOTHECA NEERLANDICA

A Library of Classics of Dutch and Flemish Literature